Artificial Intelligence and Data Mining for Mergers and Acquisitions

T0321391

Artificial Intelligence and Data Mining for Mergers and Acquisitions

Debasis Chanda

CRC Press
Taylor & Francis Group
Boca Raton London New York

CRC Press is an imprint of the
Taylor & Francis Group, an **informa** business

First edition published 2021
by CRC Press
6000 Broken Sound Parkway NW, Suite 300, Boca Raton, FL 33487-2742

and by CRC Press
2 Park Square, Milton Park, Abingdon, Oxon, OX14 4RN

CRC Press is an imprint of Taylor & Francis Group, LLC

ISBN: 978-1-138-35473-9 (hbk)
ISBN: 978-0-367-72090-2 (pbk)
ISBN: 978-0-429-42457-1 (ebk)

Typeset in Palatino
by SPi Global, India

Dedication

This book is dedicated to the loving memory of my late father, Mr. Arun Kumar Chanda, who has been a pillar of strength and inspiration all through my life, as well as my mother, Mrs. Sabita Chanda, who has always untiringly taken care of every little requirement in my life.

It is also dedicated to my spouse, Ranita, for her unwavering and unstinted support; and last but not least, to my son Debannik, who continues to teach me ways of life that I had long forgotten, through his innocence, youthful simplicity, and maturity.

Contents

Preface

The book is written primarily for the following audience: students of strategic management in business schools, post-graduate programs in technology institutes, looking for application areas of AI & data mining as well as business/technology professionals in organizations seeking to create value through M&As.

The book addresses characteristics comprising advisory for M&As of organizations (including Banks and Financial Institutions) using *fuzzy data mining framework*. Also, the book presents a new AI knowledge based process modeling framework (having well defined semantics) for creation of the virtual organization.

The unique proposition of the book lies in the novelty of the knowledge-based approach in the new domain of Service Oriented Architecture (SOA), development of an Enterprise Architectural model using AI and comparison with other modeling techniques such as Petri Nets.

Acknowledgments

First and foremost, I take this opportunity to express my gratitude to my teachers late Professor Dwijesh Dutta Majumder, Professor Emeritus, Indian Statistical Institute Kolkata and Professor Swapan Bhattacharya, former Professor, Department of Computer Science & Engineering, Jadavpur University, and former Director of National Institutes of Technology, Durgapur and Suratkal.

I also express my gratitude and thanks to Professor (Dr) Atmanand, Director, MDI Murshidabad for being my Philosopher and Guide and for the learning he has imbibed in me.

My heartfelt thanks to my very close friends, who have stuck with me through thick and thin.

My special thanks to my colleagues at MDI Murshidabad for inspiring to achieve my goals.

My special thanks to Ms. Astha Sharma of the publisher CRC Press/Taylor & Francis Group for her patience and the confidence she has reposed in me. My special thanks also to Ms. Shikha Garg for her prompt helping hand.

About the Author

Debasis Chanda is Professor of Operations Management and Dean-Academic at MDI Murshidabad, West Bengal, India. He holds a Bachelor of Engineering (Electrical Engineering) from Jadavpur University, Kolkata. He also holds a PGDBM from the Indian institute of Management Calcutta (IIMC) and a PhD (Engineering) from the Department of Computer Science and Engineering, Jadavpur University.

Professor Debasis Chanda brings forth a blend of rich experience in Industry and Academics. He has 20-plus years of cross-functional experience in the Information Technology (IT) Industry including global exposure in Enterprise Architecture Consulting, SOA (Service Oriented Architecture) Consulting, Project Management & Business Development. He also has more than five years of experience in the Engineering Industry along with more than five years in Academia.

Professor Debasis Chanda's competencies also include Operations Start-up as well as Strategizing & Brand Building.

1

Introduction

1.1 Introduction

Mergers and Acquisitions (M&As) are recurring phenomena in the global business space. This includes M&As in all industry domains, marked by pronounced activity in the space of Banking and Financial Institutions.

From the business-technology perspective, consolidation of two banks during M&A requires consolidation of business processes of the participating organizations. This requires that the participating banks act as technologically autonomous business units, so that the benefits of large-scale organizational system and small-scale organizational operations are preserved without unsettling each other.

The realization of each business process for the consolidated banking organization (following the merger of the two representative banking organizations) requires the orchestration/composition of the business processes for each of the two banking organizations into consolidated business process.

The Virtual Organization (VO) is a conceptual structure, which is in general the collaborative alliance between business associates in Value Chains (VCs), is a significant aspect for studying sustainability of organizations in the competitive business milieu to produce more competitive offerings. A VO is a temporary enterprise which is created according to a business prospect and may be wound up when the business prospect no longer exists. The VO is designed to boost competitiveness, to optimize resource use, to augment magnitude of the business, and to take benefits of the complementary capabilities of the business affiliates.

The VO is made up of higher-level VCs and each value chain is made up of the collaborative business processes for business execution in a loosely-coupled way. Each business process is regarded as the core competitive functionality of the lower-level VO and the lower-level VO repeatedly is composed of the further lower-level VCs. This composition manner among the VOs, the VCs, and the collaborative business processes is repeated recursively to the extent it is required by the system or until these cannot be divided any more. Representative modeling language is the Unified Modeling Language (UML). In the world of business, the manifestation of VOs is through M&As/JVs (Joint Ventures).

Service-oriented application software is becoming the major standard for leveraging inter-organization information systems to execute higher-level business transactions.

Web Service (WS) compositions can be achieved by using Petri nets that could facilitate a comprehensive perspective of the composed/orchestrated Web Service.

Service-Oriented Architectures (SOA) as a paradigm for interoperability of applications within and without the enterprise is gaining increased acceptance. In this methodology, distributed applications are manifested as (Web) services, which interoperate by means of WS standards.

Various approaches are advocated to deal with these challenges. Process-based service composition relates to workflow and BPM (Business Process Management).

The goal of the book is to present a modeling framework for the VO, which is focused on process composition by consolidating individual UML process models into consolidated process model. This framework uses predicate calculus knowledge bases. Petri net-based modeling of the business processes are discussed, as well. We also propose a data mining model, using a fuzzy mathematical approach, which aims to discover knowledge in banking databases and determines those candidate organizations that are suitable for merger.

1.2 Organization of the Book

The rest of this work is organized as follows: In Chapter 2 the scope of the book is articulated. In Chapter 3 we furnish literature review, which provides the scope, significance, and justification of the current work. In Chapter 4, the proposed *fuzzy data mining framework* is discussed. In Chapters 5, 6 & 7, we discuss UML-based modeling of business processes and discourse on enterprise architecture/service-oriented architecture, knowledge representation using predicate calculus and Petri net-based modeling of business processes, respectively. Finally, Chapter 8 provides some concluding remarks and scenarios where the framework can be applied.

2

Scope of the Book

2.1 Introduction

The book discusses creation of a Fuzzy Data mining Framework for creation of VO, modeling of business processes with Unified Modeling Language (UML), consolidation of individual business processes by the proposed KB (Knowledge Based) methodology and Petri Net based methodology.

The book proposes Fuzzy Cluster Analysis towards merger of banks/financial organizations and evolution of an AI (Artificial Intelligence) based (SOA) Service Oriented Architecture using representative case study to exemplify modeling of business processes during M&A (Merger & Acquisition) situation. A Knowledge Base is created, and inferences are arrived at. Goal based inferences correspond to Business Processes. Atomic business processes correspond to sub-goals. Discovery of business processes is manifested by means of Pattern Search & Unification/Substitution algorithms.

In the book we address concerns related to identification of the most appropriate candidates for M&A (Merger & Acquisition) of organizations. During the pre-merger stage, a few prospects may be on hand to go through the M&A, but all of them may possibly not be appropriate. The usual process is to take up a due diligence task to identify the contenders that should bring about best possible increase in investor worth and customer contentment, post-merger. The due diligence should be capable of determining those contenders that are inappropriate for M&A, those contenders that are reasonably appropriate, and those that are most appropriate. For realizing the above purpose, the book proposes a Fuzzy Data Mining Framework for suitability of M&A of Banks and other Financial Organizations.

Modeling business processes leveraging UML is handy for modeling static relationships, but has shortfalls for modeling dynamic features. UML notation is semiformal, lacking sound semantics. Class Diagrams, Sequence Diagrams as well as Activity Diagrams are markedly separate representations in UML without consistency and integrity checks. Petri Nets, on the other hand, though comprising formalized notations, are not useful for representing static relations, not being crafted for that objective.

A Knowledge Based framework has been proposed in the book, to present an all-inclusive knowledge store for static and dynamic properties.

The book also takes a look at a discourse on Enterprise Architecture (EA)/Service Oriented Architecture (SOA).

2.2 Objectives of the Book

The objectives of the book are:

- A Fuzzy Data Mining Framework for suitability of M&A of Banks and Financial Institutions.
- A new Predicate Calculus Knowledge based process modeling framework in the domain of Service Oriented Architecture (SOA)
- Contrast between three approaches viz. UML, Petri Nets & Predicate Calculus Knowledge Base

2.3 Conclusion

This chapter presents a broad overview of the scope, goals and contributions of the book.

3

Review of Related Work

3.1 Introduction

This chapter provides the significance of the publication, including article references available in related areas.

3.2 Architecture Centric Methodology

Application of SOA into reconfigurable supply chains are spelt out [1]. Our book adopts the SOA model to accomplish faultless technology amalgamation of Banking facilities.

Service discovery and selection by means of Service Registry is discussed [2]. Our effort puts forward Knowledge Based repository of processes/services wherein pattern search & unification/substitution discovery is manifested.

Model sharing and reuse in a distributed environment is discussed [3]. Our proposed Knowledge Base makes possible sharing/reuse in a distributed set-up.

The work by Fang et al. [4] goes over Business Process Management (BPM) and emphasizes integration of SOA technologies for joint learning in a collaborative situation. We focus on banking services and their consolidation, pertinent from BPM & SOA context.

Kim et al. [5] proposes a structure for creating responsive and interoperable VOs. The framework supports consistent enterprise representation, akin to our framework/architecture for consolidation of services that may well be taken-up enterprise-wide.

Marcos Lopez-Sanz et al. [6] put forward an architecture oriented model driven development, and depicts UML representation for Platform Independent Model (PIM)—level SOA modeling. Similarly, UML has been proposed in this work for knowledge capture.

David Chen et al. [7] outline and shed light on enterprise architecture concepts. We put forth a Knowledge Based process/service consolidation, enterprise-wide.

Collaborative networks (CNs) [8] comprise of diverse and physically dispersed enterprises with dissimilar capabilities, but complementary pursuits, which combine to realize mutual purpose. We recommend a wide-ranging interoperable Knowledge Based framework.

Karim Baına et al. [9] present dynamic diverse process interoperability. We suggest consolidation of processes during M&As (Mergers & Acquisitions).

Daniela Grigori et al. [10] present integrated tools to manage process execution quality. Similarly, we ensure execution quality by way of WFF (Well Defined Formulae).

Ricardo Jardim-Goncalves et al. [11] present model-driven architectures. We have also proposed service oriented paradigm for M&As (Mergers & Acquisitions).

Rezgui [12] discusses role based authorization for service consumption. Our proposed architecture handles authentication and authorization.

Han et al. [13] present service-oriented problem-solving scenario for bio-informatics study. We handle a service oriented scenario for Banks/Financial organizations.

The paper by Chanda et al. [14] proposes Distributed Architecture for a banking system. Nadhan [15] and Channabasavaiah et al. [16] talk about different methodologies towards implementing SOA, which is pertinent to our work.

Ram Mohan [17], Nitsure [18] provide economic viewpoints to bank M&A, also being the focus of our work.

Aslanertik [19] introduces value creation through process integration. Similarly, we focus on business processes integration of constituent organizations of VO.

Baïna et al. [20] look at modeling methodology for product information and its administration. Our work is useful in rapid turnaround of new services/products by means of lower level services.

Chao et al. [21] adopt Business Process Execution Language for Web Services (BPEL4WS) for workflow control. Our work too is business process service oriented.

Chen et al. [22] delineate the traits of a VO and VO access control. Likewise, our work also proposes access control mechanisms.

Lu et al. [23] propose a model for process interoperability. The subject work also proposes interoperability.

3.3 Petri Net Centric Business Process Modeling

Valero et al. [24] focus on Petri nets as formalism for validation systems. We deliberate service composition with Petri Nets in our work.

Ouyang et al. [25] present mapping of BPEL constructs onto Petri net configuration. Static and dynamic system models are mapped into Petri net configuration in our work.

Lohmann et al. [26] analyze the communication between business processes, and translation to Petri net model. Likewise, we translate processes into Petri nets.

Backer et al. [27] delve into Petri Net based verification for interoperable business processes. Petri Nets models are used for modeling interoperable business processes in the subject work.

Bastide et al. [28] look at Coloured Petri nets based formal semantics. Our work, while considering Petri Net based modeling, considers formal semantics based on Knowledge Bases.

Cheung et al. [29] apply use-case based design. We also consider use case based processes/services.

Ehrig et al. [30] look at rule-based methodology for dynamic transformations. Our subject work considers rule-based expert systems.

Gasevic et al. [31] put forth Petri net ontology to facilitate sharing Petri nets Web 3.0. Our work looks at UML, Petri Nets and Knowledge Bases.

Ha et al. [32] deliberate soundness /properties of PWF-nets. Our work also looks at business processes/workflows.

Julia et al. [33] propose a p-time Petri net based approach to explain real time scheduling concerns of Workflow Management. Token player algorithm is applied to defined order of tasks respecting time constraints. Our subject looks at token propagation for manifesting business processes/workflows.

Wil M.P. van der Aalst [34] puts forth frameworks for manifestation of workflow systems using Petri nets. Petri Nets is one of the frameworks handled in our work.

Russell et al. [35] put forth review of control-flow patterns in the shape of Coloured Petri-Net (CPN), as well as. business process modeling formalisms, relevant to our subject work.

Wil van der Aalst et al. [36] discuss business-management context within which work-flow management systems operate, as well as analyzes processes and models; in our work we analyze processes.

Ding et al. [37] infer that it is simpler to put into practice a discrete-FTPN (Fuzzy Time Petri Net) model, however for a academic research the continuous-FTPN model is better. Our work looks at conventional Petri Net models.

Padberg et al. [38] combine the concepts of Petri net modules (Padberg [39]), and component framework for system modeling (Ehrig et al. [40]). Our subject work also considers Petri Net based framework wherein some atomic business processes may be deemed as generic components.

Rosa-Velardo et al. [41] represent devices/apparatus and software components as portable coloured Petri Nets. Likewise, we consider a service oriented Petri Net.

3.4 UML Centric Business Process Modeling

Rambaugh et al. [42] and Priestley [43] look at Object Oriented Modeling as well as UML (Unified Modeling Language), also being an approach adopted in our subject work.

HJ Koehler, U Nickel, J Niere, A Zuendorf [44] suggest use of UML static structure and interaction diagrams for visual representation. Our subject work adopts UML diagrams for consolidation of processes/services.

UML notions from Wikipedia [45] has been adopted in our work.

Andersson et al. [46] look at how Unified Modeling Language could be used with SDL (Specification & Description Language) formalized by the ITU (International Telecommunication Union). We use UML diagrams to articulate applications in the form of predicate calculus.

Akhlaki et al. [47] aim at assimilate UML collaboration diagram for temporal requirements integration. Our work uses Petri Nets, which are designed to handle temporal modeling requirements.

Berardi et al. [48] consider UML class diagrams, which are one of the most important components of UML, and address the problem of Knowledge Representation and Reasoning. We also consider Predicate Logic and UML & Petri Nets based Knowledge Representation.

Berkenk¨otter [49] puts forth that Unified Modeling Language as is not capable of ensuring validation of models and strengthens UML by extension. Our work looks at improvement of UML using Predicate Calculus.

Borges et al. [50] integrate UML class diagrams and the formal specification language OhCircus. Our work uses Predicate Calculus to put across knowledge expressed through UML by means of WFF (Well Formed Formulae).

Thouraya Bouabana-Tebibel [51] look at automating formal validation of performance of systems depicted in UML. Our proposed Knowledge Based model caters to static and dynamic semantics.

Ferreira et al. [52] present models wherein they explain both static and dynamic perspectives of a system. In our work, Predicate Calculus describes both static and dynamic perspectives of a system.

Glezer et al. [53] report that UML Collaboration Diagrams are easier to figure out than Sequence Diagrams in Real Time systems, but there is no differentiation in understanding of the two diagram categories in MIS. In our work, which is in the area of MIS applications, Sequence Diagrams are used for modeling.

Grossman et al. [54] indicate a wide diversity of opinion regarding UML adoption, depicting the relative debate over its usefulness. We use Unified Modeling Language (UML) for depicting business processes.

Ho¨ lscher et al. [55] provides an approach towards formal semantics for Unified Modeling Language (UML). Our Predicate Calculus Knowledge Bases use WFF (Well Formed Formulae).

Ali Kamandi et al. [56] put forth transformation methods for important notions and diagrams of UML into OSANs (object stochastic activity networks). In our work we use and perform comparative study of UML and Petri Net techniques.

Kong [57] et al. propose a graphical and formal approach denoting semantics of statechart diagrams. Petri Nets and Predicate Calculus Knowledge Bases are used in our work to capture behavioral semantics.

Lucas et al. [58] identify issues, trends and future research regarding UML model consistency management. We look at formal Knowledge Based representation, whereas UML is semi-formal.

Previous research has revealed that technique and rigor used in UML representations differ extensively across software assignments [59-61]. Nugroho [62] assesses thoroughness in UML modeling. We propose Knowledge Based model (formal model) to surmount drawbacks that arise on account of semi-formality of UML.

Ziemann et al. [63] look at corroboration of UML models by way of graph transformation. They focus on statechart and collaboration diagrams. We use Class Diagrams and Sequence Diagrams (comparableto Collaboration Diagrams).

3.5 Knowledge Based Methodology

Claus Pahl [64] proposes reasoning methods for semantic service architecture. This is corresponding to our subject work wherein UML based modeling technique is adopted, along with Knowledge Based framework for business processes/services consolidation.

Arroyo et al. [65] discuss semantic service-oriented choreography. Our work proposes consolidation/choreography adopting semantic Knowledge Bases.

Jagdev et al. [66] discuss semantic web services technologies and execution environment. We suggest syntactically and semantically correct Well Formed Formulae (WFF).

Jung et al. [67] discuss integration of BPMSs (Business Process Management Systems) and KMSs (Knowledge Management Systems). Our work also looks at knowledge bases and business processes.

Luger [68] expounds the spirit of AI (Artificial Intelligence)—unraveling complex problems related to computer technology. In our work AI (Artificial Intelligence) concepts are applied towards knowledge base development.

Dirk Beyer et al. [69] discuss manipulation of relations based on predicate calculus. Our work discusses predicate calculus for creation of knowledge bases.

Chen [70] researches innovation methodologies for accomplishment of knowledge-oriented networks. Likewise, our subject work considers Knowledge Bases.

Samara et al. [71] incorporate knowledge base traits for clinical setting. Our work looks at Knowledge Bases in the Banking area.

Rodriguez et al. [72] propose knowledge based CPD (collaborative product development). We, in our work, also propose Knowledge Based Model.

Chanda et al. [73] put forth a suitable approach for consolidation of static structure and interaction diagrams. They have used an AI (Artificial Intelligence) oriented approach.

Chanda et al. [74,75] have proposed virtual consolidation for merger/acquisition of banks/financial institutions.

Chanda et al. [76] discuss modeling of business processes during Mergers & Acquisitions (M&As) of organizations, using Knowledge Bases.

Chanda et al. [77] address concerns regarding identification of appropriate contenders for Merger & Acquisition (M&A) of Banks and Financial Institutions.

3.6 Fuzzy Logic Based Methodology

Simha et al. [78] analyze customer loyalty using fuzzy context model. Fuzzy linguistic variables are used in our work, Chen et al. [79] utilize fuzzy data mining method to establish association rules regarding web preference of customers. Our work uses fuzzy data mining methodology to establish association rules in banking domain.

Subramanyam et al. [80] put forth a fuzzy data mining model for mining of patterns from databases. We, in our work, apply fuzzy data mining algorithms.

Han [81] deliberates data mining notions and method. The same is pertinent to our subject work.

Yang [82] studies complexity analysis to data mining problems dealing with complex data structures. We look at data mining data from transactional records.

Jin et al. [83] use fuzzy similar matrix methods to intrusion detection systems. Our work proposes fuzzy clustering for mining of banking records.

Tai et al. [84] combine fuzzy sets and data mining methodology to propose a preference perception system. We propose fuzzy data mining with respect to Mergers & Acquisitions (M&As).

Bernadette Bouchon-Meunier [85] provide tools to recognize alike or unlike description of items. We put forth real-world terms for mining of banking databases.

Hu [86] suggest fuzzy if-then classification rules with genetic algorithm in high dimensional character space. Our work looks at high dimensional banking data.

Huang et al. [87] proposes a knowledge discovery model for efficient discovery of knowledge in fuzzy databases. We put forth analysis applying fuzzy data mining.

Ghazavi et al. [88] use fuzzy data mining for study of medical information. We suggest mining of high dimensional banking records.

Angryk [89] investigates distance-based fuzzy relational database. In our work, we look at fuzzy relational databases.

Chiang et al. [90] suggest fuzzy linguistic approach, similar to our proposed system which takes up fuzzy linguistic methodology.

Dutta Majumder et al. [91,92] use a fuzzy set methodology for agricultural databases to discover knowledge, which is pertinent to our work that looks at knowledge discovery in the context of banking systems.

Dutta Majumder et al. [93], Klir et al. [94], Adriaans et al. [95] and Silberschatz et al. [96] furnish notions on fuzzy mathematics, databases and data mining, the theme of our subject work.

The Annual Report [97] consists of banking reports viz. Balance Sheet and Profit & Loss Account referred to in our work.

3.7 Conclusion

In this chapter works related to the scope of work have been reviewed. The works reviewed are with respect to Architecture Centric Methodology, Petri Net Centric Business Process Modeling, UML Centric Business Process Modeling, Knowledge Based Methodology and Fuzzy Logic Based Methodology. In the next chapter, we discuss Fuzzy Logic Based Methodology.

4

Fuzzy Datamining Framework for Creation of Virtual Organization

4.1 Introduction

In this chapter we address the identification of suitable contenders for Mergers. In the pre-merger period, some contenders may be on hand to go through the M&A, however every one of them may possibly not be appropriate. The standard procedure is to perform due diligence to determine the contenders that leads to best possible enhancement in investor worth and patron fulfillment, post-merger. The due diligence should be to identify those contenders which are unbefitting of M&A, contenders that are reasonably appropriate, and contenders that are for the most part appropriate. Toward attaining the above purpose, a Fuzzy Data Mining Framework has been proposed.

4.2 Banking System Case Study: Reports (Table 4.1)

TABLE 4.1

Banking System Reports

Report	Relations	Attributes
Balance Sheet	Capital and Liabilities	• Capital • Reserves and Surplus • Deposits • Borrowings • Other Liabilities and Provisions
	Assets	• Cash & Balances with Central Bank • Balances with Banks & Money at Call and Short Notice • Investments • Advances • Fixed Assets • Other Assets
	Income	• Interest earned • Other income
	Expenditure	• Interest Expended • Operating Expenses • Provisions & Contingencies • Net Profit/(Loss) for the year

Profit & Loss Account	Net Profit	• Add: Profit/(Loss) brought forward
		• Appropriations
		  • Transfer to Statutory Reserve Transfer to Capital Reserve
		  • Transfer to Revenue and other Reserves Balance carried over to Balance Sheet

4.3 Fuzzy Data Mining Framework

4.3.1 Fuzzy Cluster Analysis

A banking organization may be expressed by the relations in Section 4.2. The attributes of the relations may be articulated by fuzzy linguistic variables Very low, Low, Medium, High and Very High, represented by an integer set {1,2,3,4,5}. Thus, points in multidimensional space represent records. We define a fuzzy compatibility relation R (reflexive and symmetric), using the Minkowski distance function for all pairs

$$\langle x_i, x_k \rangle \in X$$

where R is the set of all non-negative real numbers. δ(Inverse of the largest distance in X) is a constant that makes sure that $R(x_i, x_k) \in [0,1]$.

Where $q \in R^+$ (the set of all non-negative real numbers)

As an example, we make use of a small data set, using integer sets equivalent to fuzzy linguistic variables,

$$R(x_i, x_k) = 1 - \delta \left(\sum_{j=1}^{p} |x_{ij} - x_{kj}|^q \right)^{1/q}$$

involving five points in R^2, illustrated in Table 4.2.

Where say X_{k1} depicts Investments, and X_{k2} depicts Advances.

For q=2 (Euclidean distance), the largest Euclidean distance among any pair of coordinates is 4 (between x_1 and x_5). Therefore, δ=1/4=0.25. Thus,

$$R(x_1, x_3) = 1 - 0.25 \left\{ (3-1)^2 + (4-1)^2 \right\}^{0.5} = 0.1$$

TABLE 4.2

Representative Data Set

K	1	2	3	4	5
X_{k1}	1	2	3	4	5
X_{k2}	1	2	4	2	1

$$R = \begin{bmatrix} 1 & .65 & .1 & .21 & 0 \\ .65 & 1 & .44 & .5 & .21 \\ .1 & .44 & 1 & .44 & .1 \\ .21 & .5 & .44 & 1 & .65 \\ 0 & .21 & .1 & .65 & 1 \end{bmatrix}$$

The transitive closure is

$$R_T = \begin{bmatrix} 1 & .65 & .44 & .5 & .5 \\ .65 & 1 & .44 & .5 & .5 \\ .44 & .44 & 1 & .44 & .44 \\ .5 & .5 & .44 & 1 & .65 \\ .5 & .5 & .44 & .65 & 1 \end{bmatrix}$$

There are four distinct partitions of its α-cuts:

$$\alpha \in [0, .44] : \{ \{ x_1, x_2, x_3, x_4, x_5 \} \}$$
$$\alpha \in [.44, .5] : \{ \{ x_1, x_2, x_4, x_5 \}, \{ x_3 \} \}$$
$$\alpha \in [.5, .65] : \{ \{ x_1, x_2 \}, \{ x_3 \}, \{ x_4, x_5 \} \}$$
$$\alpha \in [.65, 1] : \{ \{ x_1 \}, \{ x_2 \}, \{ x_3 \}, \{ x_4 \}, \{ x_5 \} \}$$

The cluster tree for Euclidean distance is as follows

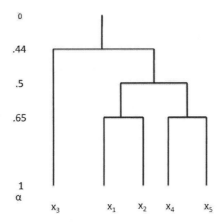

There is close association between points (x_1, x_2) and between points (x_4, x_5).

Multidimensional (with multiple attributes) clustering is also possible. Organizations in unlike-clusters complement each other, and are suitable contenders for consolidation / merger. Conversely, in the event contender organizations belong to same cluster, they are not the appropriate contenders.

4.4 Fuzzy Data Mining with Relational Databases

Following are fuzzy relations, using integer set mentioned in the foregoing.

Table 4.3 is illustrated by the attributes organization_id and organization_ name.

The relation financial_statement represents Balance Sheet attributes (Table 4.4). The primary key is combination of organization_id and the financial_year.

The relation regional_access (Table 4.5) is about regional penetration (such as the number of branches) of the banking organization.

TABLE 4.3

Relation *organization_name*

organization_id	organization_name
1	Banking_Organization1
2	Banking_Organization2
3	
4	

TABLE 4.4

Relation *financial_statement*

organization_id	financial_year	feature_1	feature_2	feature_3
1	2017	5	2	3
2	2017	4	1	5
3	2017	4	4	4
4	2017	2	3	5

TABLE 4.5

Relation *regional_access*

organization_id	financial_year	region_1	region_2	region_3
1	2017	5	1	4
2	2017	2	3	2
3	2017	1	5	2
4	2017	4	2	1

TABLE 4.6

Fuzzy Compatibility Relation

	5	4	3	2	1
5	1	.8	.6	.4	.2
4	.8	1	.8	.6	.4
3	.6	.8	1	.8	.6
2	.4	.6	.8	1	.8
1	.2	.4	.6	.8	1

The illustrative fuzzy compatibility relation is shown in Table 4.6.
The relation is defined on the nearness of regions to the reference region.

A representative query could be: "For year 2017, identify alike banking organizations with similar access in region_1."

This is the join on the relations "organization_name", "financial_statement" and "regional_access " on the attribute organization_id, for region_1 and financial_year=2017, threshold feature_1 (such as assets) $\geq$.6 and threshold access for region_1$\geq$.8.

The outcome relation is shown in Table 4.7.

It is seen that organization1 and organization2 assets i.e. feature_1are alike i.e. > threshold of 0.6 (reference to the fuzzy compatibility relation, compatibility of 5 with 4 is.8; compatibility of 5 with 2 is.4). For organization_id 1 the threshold regional_access for geog_1 $\geq$.8 (as the compatibility of 5 with 5 as perceived from the fuzzy compatibility relation is 1; compatibility of 5 with 2 is.4), as shown in Table 4.8.

The aforementioned approach facilitates derivation of association rules. One can thus determine the candidate banks which would be most appropriate for the M&A.

TABLE 4.7

Query Response

organization_id	feature_1	region_1
1	5	5
2	4	2
3	4	2
4	2	4

TABLE 4.8

Outcome of Query

organization_id	asset
1	5

4.5 Benefits of the Proposed Method

4.5.1 Extraction of Realistic Hidden Patterns

The discussed methodology uses real world terminology (linguistic variables) in comparison to crisp set based classical approach, and thus realistic.

4.5.2 Outlier Analysis

Information objects, not complying with the general representation of data, and widely dissimilar to the remaining dataset, are outliers, and might be of noteworthy attention.

4.5.3 Augmented Insights

Augmented insights are possible with fuzzy relational approach, not realizable in classical approach.

4.5.4 More Generalized Method

Methodologies created with crisp methodology can be catered to by fuzzy methodology.

4.6 Conclusion

The Fuzzy Mathematical Model enables decision makers to manage operations effectively, optimize total cost of operations and also assess the M&As of organizations.

5

UML Based Modeling of Business Processes & Discourse on Enterprise Architecture (EA)/Service Oriented Architecture (SOA)

5.1 Introduction

The representative area discussed is the business as usual of two banking organizations namely Banking_Organization1 and Banking_Organization2. The illustrative use case 'show funds' has been considered for both banking organizations.

For the use case 'show funds', the events are:

i. Client (Actor) provides Account Number
ii. Interface returns available funds for the subject Account Number

5.2 Knowledge Representation using UML (Unified Modeling Language)

The UML diagrams provided are Figure 5.1 and Figure 5.2 (class diagrams), and Figure 5.3 and Figure 5.4 (sequence diagrams). Sequence diagrams Figure 5.3 and Figure 5.4 represent the processes 'show funds' for Banking_Organization1 and Banking_Organization2, illustrating the passing of messages among objects. In SOA (Service Oriented Architecture) parlance, the process 'show funds' is a 'Service'.

The client's request to show the available funds for a Bank Account Number passes the relevant Bank Account Number as parameter. The response from the system is the available funds in the account.

For Banking_Organization1, the client passes the Bank Account Number to the controller object (object of the Banking_Organization class). This object manages and synchronizes the responses (Figure 5.3).

The controller object on receiving the Bank Account Number passed to it, initiates a new activation, by communicating to the object that maintains the set of accounts, which finally results in a response back to the Client.

Figure 5.3 illustrates the System class that connects to all accounts. It searches for and reverts with the required account information.

The system object obtains the Bank Account Number of every account object and subsequently sends back the Bank Account Number corresponding to the Bank Account

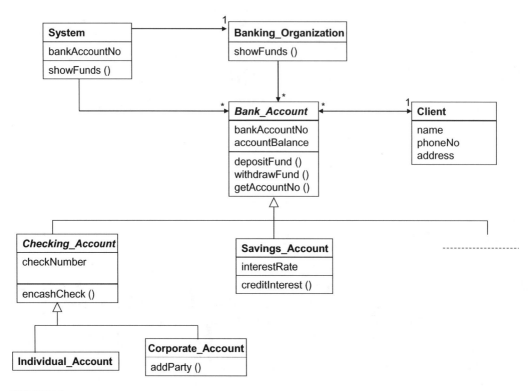

FIGURE 5.1
Class Diagram for Banking_Organization1.

Number passed in the request. The communication would be sent several times to a range of Bank_Account objects.

The association from the System class (Figure 5.1: Banking_Organization1 class diagram) to the Bank_Account class shows that the System class keeps information of all bank accounts. Bank accounts are represented by separate class instances. The System class keeps track of the bank accounts by maintaining linkage to every bank account.

The messages in the sequence diagram rematerialize as operations in classes in the class diagram.

For the Banking_Organization object, the business necessity is to record that clients have bank accounts. The Client class has attributes phone number and address. Every bank account belongs to a client, and every client may possess multiple bank accounts.

The Bank_Account class portrays the common characteristics of child classes, that is, the Checking_Account and Savings_Account. The Bank Account class is an abstract class (nonexistent). The Individual_Account and Corporate_Account are subclasses of Checking_ Account. Bank_Account class has attributes 'bankAccountNo' and 'accountBalance' and the operations 'depositFund', 'getAccountNo' and 'withdrawFund' are inherited by subclasses.

The Checking_Account subclass records check numbers in a check book, with operation 'encashCheck'.

Corporate_Accounts are operated by corporates with operation to add anotherparty ('addParty').

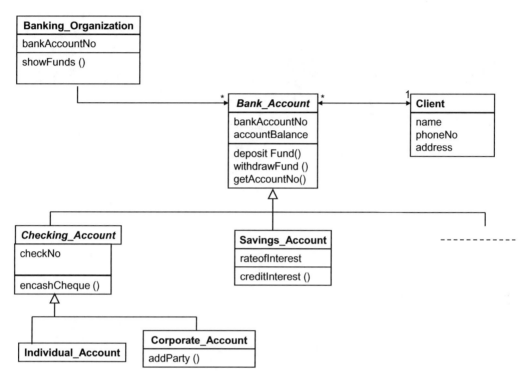

FIGURE 5.2
Class Diagram for Banking_Organization2.

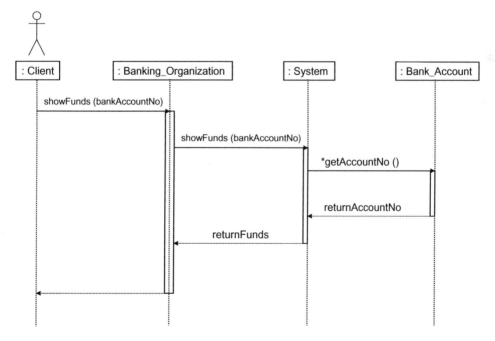

FIGURE 5.3
Sequence Diagram for showFunds: Banking_Organization1.

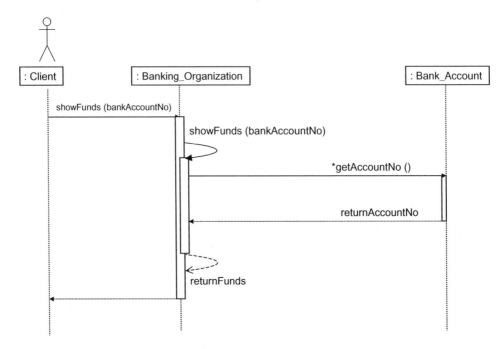

FIGURE 5.4
Sequence Diagram for showFunds: Banking_Organization2.

The Banking_Organization class has one to one association with System class and one too many associations with the Bank_Account class. The System class has one too many associations with Bank_Account class.

There is, however, an essential difference in Banking_Organization2 design. For Banking_Organization2, the Banking_Organization object (Figure 5.4) is the controller, and also maintains information of Bank_Account business objects as represented in Figure 5.2, (class diagram for Banking_Organization2).

5.3 Discourse on Enterprise Architecture (EA)/Service Oriented Architecture (SOA)

5.3.1 About Enterprise Architecture

This discourse presents the representative architecture ecosystem view for an enterprise, as envisioned to realize the goals and strategic objectives laid out by the executive leadership team of an enterprise. The definition has been guided by the Architecture Principles laid out.

The architecture envisioning takes an approach driven by set of architecture models. It defines a Platform—Independent logical/conceptual Model (Platform Independent Model—PIM).

The discourse provides a brief narration for the different architectural layers and building blocks of the architecture (referred formally as Architecture Building Blocks or ABBs) within such layers as depicted in the architecture diagram. It provides an overview of the building blocks and explains the responsibility area for these blocks. The discourse looks at the architecture from the perspective of a few selected process areas (also referred in the report as Theme areas). Examples of such Theme areas include Order Management, Financial Management, Rights and Royalties, Business Intelligence (BI) & Reporting, Product Management, Content Management System (CMS), Customer Relationship Management (CRM) and Sales.

5.3.2 Introduction

This discourse summarizes the envisioned Future State Architecture.

The architecture is driven by Vision, Strategic Objectives and draws upon Industry Best Practices and Experience. It is guided by Architecture Principles defined.

5.3.3 Architecture Definition Approach

The future state architecture has been developed to provide a framework that helps attain the capabilities identified for fulfilling the organization's Strategic Objectives, Architecture Considerations for Guiding Principles and Capabilities.

The following section summarizes some specific considerations made while defining the architecture to stay aligned with the guiding Architecture Principles and reinforce these principles into the solution that may be built conforming to this architecture.

5.3.3.1 Enterprise Architecture Principles

Table 5.1 provides an outline of how the architecture has been guided by the Architecture Principles.

5.3.3.2 Strategic Objectives

The Strategic Objectives would be realized through the solution implementation in its entirety. However, the future state enterprise architecture, even at the level of abstraction appropriate for that perspective and current level of detailing, makes some specific design choices toward the realization of the same.

The following Strategic Objectives are kept in conscious consideration while envisioning the representative architecture:

1. Digital Enablement
2. Customer Focus
3. Process & Resource Harmonization
4. Technology Excellence
5. Services Growth
6. Geographic Expansion
7. Market Expansion
8. Strategic Partnerships

The service-based paradigm set by the Architecture Principle, is now accepted in the industry to bring in overall efficiency and agility to the enterprise allowing for a plug-and-play model of solution development. It allows for superior levels of modularization of the solution with

TABLE 5.1

Enterprise Architecture Principles

Architecture Principle	Future State Architecture Considerations
Prefer Use over Buy over Build	The architecture elaboration is clearly separated into platform independent and platform specific considerations to prepare the ground for this. Once the Architecture Building Blocks (ABB) are identified as part of the conceptual/logical architecture (PIM), the selection of solution options is further expected to leverage this principle
Set up Enterprise Solutions with Local Variants	The architecture provides a common enterprise architecture framework that can be used to harmonize around. The Theme specific perspectives set the stage up for taking individual scenarios and designing for common enterprise solutions with necessary variants that have justifications to differ
Drive for Reusable Solution Building Blocks	Reuse is driven into the design by defining ABBs upfront with clear responsibility areas for reuse across the enterprise. Integration Infrastructure is designed to allow for reuse of services provided by these ABBs across the enterprise. When solution options are mapped it is expected that individual solutions are mapped to their responsibility areas to enforce the drive toward reuse. Detailed requirements analysis may identify areas for local variants
Avoid Current State Driving/Constraining Future State Design	The envisioned architecture is designed without being dragged backward by any existing design. Using this as reference for future architecture detailing helps to ensure that future architecture in its elaborated state also remains forward looking
Delineate Architectural Responsibility	The future state architecture has clearly delineated architectural responsibility into layers. ABBs with both functional as well as technology affinity are also marked to serve the same objective
Base Architecture on Service Orientation	The architecture is designed using service orientation principles and specific layers are depicted like for business and information: data services
Comply to Standards	The architecture is defined complying with general architecture standards and best practices
Rationalize Technology	Architecture provides a common reference and the section on PSM (Platform Specific Model) deliberates on technology selections. It does not step into the area of rationalizing technology
Maintain Gold Copy of Data	The architecture lays out clearly demarcated information: data services layer and shows repository for key business/domain/enterprise entities. It lays down the framework for superior integration that is essential for different services/systems/applications to collaborate to abide by this principle
Share Responsibility toward Objectives	The architecture is designed with ABBs with clear responsibility areas. The framework laid out for integration, sets the stage for ABBs to collaborate while fulfilling a shared responsibility toward objective
Reduce Manual Interventions	Various layers and ABBs work together toward fulfillment of this objective. The orchestration layer plays a key role
Secure Information	At the ecosystem view level, clearly marked ABBs is designed to cover for security reasons

distinct architecture building blocks providing set of services based on their individual responsibility areas. These services are orchestrated for fulfillment of higher business goals. The shift from development and re-development way of life to one where solutions can be built by composition through reuse of existing services is a key tenet here. All these help contribute to several of the strategic objectives listed above. Needless to say, the most direct relationship of the entire architecture definition is toward the fulfillment of the Strategic Objective of **Technology Excellence**. The overall paradigm is recognized in the technology industry and across business domains to enable specific Strategic Objectives on **Services Growth**, **Geographic Extension** and **Market Expansion** leveraging the characteristics described above.

For helping to realize the Strategic Objectives for **Digital Enablement**, clearly demarcated channels are defined. These include web browsers, mobile apps, eReaders, tablets, etc. Digital enablement is seen to require higher degree of fluidity in terms of information flow and efficient integration frameworks are defined both for internal as well as partner and vendor systems.

For supporting the Strategic Objective of **Customer Focus**, the architecture envisages a model where different customer-focused Architecture Building Blocks and Services in particular bring in specific capabilities for the fulfillment of this objective. In this model, different touch-points with the customers are integrated in a way to promote seamless flow of information. This enables bringing in customer focus in different aspects of the organization's operations. The architecture demarcates building block in different layers. It starts from a Consumer layer for different types of customers, provides for a Portal/Presentation layer for different views necessary to support various customer needs. This is followed by process layer for customer-focused processes. The business service layer houses all business services—not limiting to CRM but all that would need to bring in capabilities for enhanced customer focus.

For example, improved product/service quality is possible as repeated use of mature services mean proportion of new elements in a new product being launched is reduced while achieving faster time-to-market. Over a period of time, operating cost, change management impact, implementation risks and costs are all expected to come down non-trivially. The availability of a superior framework of architecture that is designed for collaboration of disparate services working toward a common goal also helps the reduction of time-to-market for new products. This in turn helps control cost, increase revenue and reduce technology risks associated with launch of new products and services enabling differentiating capabilities for the enterprise.

The primary layer for the Strategic Objective of **Process Harmonization** is the Process/Orchestration layer. The layer has ABBs categorized by Process Areas (Value Streams) and aims to let similar processes nucleate around such areas as a first step toward single instances of harmonized processes with very carefully managed variants and extensions. **Resource Harmonization** across all layers is addressed in a similar way in the architecture with clearly defined ABBs with specific responsibilities. The idea again is first recognizing at a logical/conceptual level the presence of a single logical instance of a particular responsibility area and then detail out the responsibilities and services in a way that is addresses similar requirements through harmonized designs (along with controlled variants and extensions).

The architecture sets in place integration infrastructure to connect with partners and vendors for seamless information flow and service invocation contributing to the fulfillment of the Strategic Objective of **Strategic Partnerships.**

5.3.3.3 Business Capabilities

Table 5.2 describes representative business capabilities and its subcomponent.

TABLE 5.2

Business Capability Areas

Business Capability Area	Business Capability	Future State Architecture Considerations
1. Dynamic Content Management	1.1 Content management repository Enterprise-wide	Architecture Building Block for Content Information Service area is defined in the Enterprise Information Service layer
	1.2 Product development workflow which is medium-agnostic	Architecture Building Blocks for Product Creation including Product Strategy and Product Proposal & Setup is defined in the Process Orchestration Layer
	1.3 Content management processes reflecting desired customer experience	Generally, customer service area is demarcated from content management and design set in place for mutual collaboration, influence and orchestrations of those
2. Product Localization	2.1 Localized user experience	Extending the above point, content is by design separated out from channels of distribution to allow them to vary independently as required
	2.2 Content translated into appropriate local languages as demanded by market	These capabilities are expected to be brought out by content services and operations
3. Flexible Pricing and Quoting	3.1 Flexible, automated promotion and pricing	Architecture building blocks for Promotion and Pricing is defined and specific flexibility will be ingrained in the service capabilities of these
	3.2 Workflow to manage pricing from price creation to quote to order to invoicing	Architecture building block for workflow is created in the orchestration
4. Enterprise Content and Service Bundling	4.1 Combined content and services for unique offerings within and across Global Business Units	The architecture envisages all products to be managed by the Architecture building block for Product Management. This is likely to collaborate with other building blocks for Content as appropriate for content-based products
	4.2 Financial processes supporting content/service bundles	Would be handled by Architecture building block defined for Financial Management and relevant orchestration layer building block/s
5. Enterprise Customer Care	5.1 Enterprise-wide, customer care appropriate to each product type and medium	Enterprise customer care like any other functional area will be addressed through several layers defined in the architecture. Customer touch points in the access/Interaction channels, Portal/ Presentation layer, Process Orchestration Layer, Business Service as well as Enterprise Information Service layer will all play key roles. These building blocks will collaborate with others as needed as well
6. 360° Enterprise Customer View	6.1 Capture enterprise-wide view of customer including all of their interactions	The capturing part will be largely start from the access channels and Portal/Presentation layer but will touch upon all layers & blocks noted above as well
	6.2 Support direct relationship with user	As above

TABLE 5.2

(Continued)

Business Capability Area	Business Capability	Future State Architecture Considerations
7. New Product Time-to-Market and Performance Measurement	7.1 Support for market/ geography research, opportunity identification and business case/model development	This area is seen to fall within the purview of the following building blocks namely Product Creation from the Process Orchestration Layer and Product Management from the business service layer. Business Analytics is a Shared Service building block that is seen to play a key role as well
	7.2 Support for rapid prototyping, piloting and evaluation of new products and services including user-centered design	Achieved through the overall architecture which is set for agility and progressively developing new products through compositions of reusable services over new developments
	7.3 Product and program performance and lifecycle management	Key building blocks identified for these include Product Creation from the orchestration layer and Product Management from the business service layer
8. Enterprise Strategic Sourcing and Vendor Management	8.1 Enterprise harmonization of sourcing, vendor selection, procurement, implementation and transition	A dedicated building block for Procurement and Vendor Management from the business service layer covers this area. The services from this area are orchestrated by Vendor Management & Procurement orchestration service from the Business Service area of Process/Orchestration layer
	8.2 Enterprise-wide performance-based vendor management including consistent measurement and reporting	Same as above
9. Enterprise Partnership Management	9.1 Identification of capabilities and business models appropriate for partnering as well as partner selection	Same As above
	9.2 Enterprise approach to partner piloting, implementation and integration	Same As above
	9.3 Enterprise processes for consistent partner relationship management	Same As above
10. Enterprise Technology Planning and Cost-effective Operation	10.1 Develop, refine, communicate and execute enterprise technology strategy and execution	No automation plans are clearly defined in the architecture for the Technology Planning and therefore no building block for the same present in the Process/Orchestration layer for the same. If there is a plan, a building block for the same would have to be defined within the Business Support area. However, business analytics can provide key analysis for such planning

5.3.4 Representative Enterprise Architecture (EA)/Service Oriented Architecture (SOA)

5.3.4.1 Representative Architectural Layers

Figure 5.5 provides a representation of different layers and tiers envisaged to define the architecture at the highest level.

Future state enterprise architecture has been constituted with multiple layers to serve different areas of responsibility. The layers are broadly classified as listed below:

- Consumers: Includes users who can access the IT systems.
- Access/Interaction channels: Includes various channels/mediums/devices that may be used by the consumers to interact with the IT systems.
- Presentation/Portal: Includes vertical portals (provide specific functionality—e.g. CRM, Order Management) and horizontal portals (provide cross cutting functionality—e.g. Customer Care, HR, Corporate Intranet).
- Process Orchestration: Includes business processes from value stream perspective.
- Business Services: Includes candidate business services that would help to realize the business processes.
- Enterprise Information: Includes information systems (RDBMS, FILE, unstructured data) that have business entities exposed as information services. These services would be consumed by business, process, presentation, data, integration and foundation services to ensure that the information is retrieved from single source of truth.
- Integration Layer: Includes integration services, adaptors, routing, transformation, validators, splitters, message handlers and acts as common gateway for external application interactions.
- Frameworks: Includes common frameworks that need to be enforced at enterprise level to enable standardization, architecture and design patterns and consistency.
- Technology Services: Includes reusable services that helps to enforce standardization, architecture and design patterns and consistency.

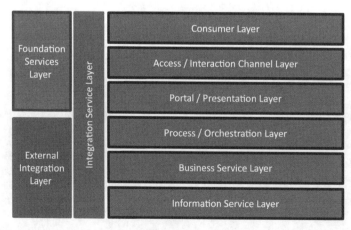

FIGURE 5.5
Representative Enterprise Architecture Layers and Tiers View.

- Foundation Platforms: Includes shared runtime and development platforms as well as reusable services exposed as part of its platform.
- External Applications: Includes Partners, Vendors, External Services, Content Providers, Content Consumers.

The following sections describe the above layers in more detail covering the responsibilities of each of the layers and significant architecture building blocks for the individual layers.

5.3.4.2 Consumers

Consumers include various user entities that interact with IT system through multiple mediums/such as web browsers, mobile, tablet devices, etc. The consumers are broadly classified as below (Table 5.3).

- Internal Users
- External Users
- Partner/Vendors Users

5.3.4.3 Access/Interaction Channels

This layer represents set of clients, devices, and channels which can be used to interact with the IT Systems. Examples of such channels include web browser client, mobile devices, tablets, etc.

5.3.4.4 Portal/Presentation

This layer represents set of presentation components which can be specific to the need of line of business, user roles, enterprise-wide and more. Abstracts and separates out the portal/presentation services from business logics for improving the separation of concern (Table 5.4).

Common portal platform encapsulates the backend business applications to the user which enables lesser impact to user experience during application transformation. Portal platform can consume business services and data services via integration layer to promote loose coupling.

Portal platform can leverage common foundation services like authentication, authorization, enterprise search, and UI personalization to enforce standardization and reuse.

TABLE 5.3

Consumer Categories

Consumer Category	Description
Internal Users	Entities/Roles who belong to the organization are considered as internal users
External Users	Entities/Roles who does not belong to the organization are considered as external users
Partner/Vendor Users	Entities/Roles who belong to Partners/Vendors are considered as Partner/Vendor users

TABLE 5.4

Portal Types

Portal Type	Description	Example
LOB or Vertical Portal	Portal which is built specific to need of a Line of Business or Vertical	CRM, Finance, Sales, Product Management, Warehouse and more. Product specific portal like salesforce.com
Personalized User Portal	Vertical portal which behaves/personalizes according to the role or profile of user	Customer care portal which behaves differently based on location, language, and product. Role-based Content management portal
Enterprise or Horizontal Portal	Portal to provide services to whole enterprise	Corporate intranet portal which provides common services like corporate communication, compliance policies & HR related information to all employees

5.3.4.5 Process/Orchestration

This layer comprises of business aligned process for a specific domain (owned/managed by different business units/departments) that are of relevance from the users' perspective. These services may be realized using orchestration of relevant services or composite services.

Process services provide unique functionality that can be leveraged by service consumers such as external clients and internal applications. It acts as business façade layer through which business services are called to reduce the network calls between portal/presentation layer and business layer.

These process services support runtime discovery of business services and agility based on defined business rules.

Process services can leverage common foundation services like rules management and auditing services via integration layer.

Table 5.5 lists business process services that form the architecture building blocks within this layer. The listed business processes are illustrative in nature.

5.3.4.6 Business Service Layer

The business services refer to the business functions (e.g. customer management, contract management, and order management) acting as building blocks of business processes. They are the highest level of abstraction of business functions (Level 1) that will use Level 2, Level 3 composite and atomic business functions. Business Functions are realized using orchestration of multiple low-level domain business services (Level 2, 3, n). They are consumed by portal/presentation layer, business process layer, and Integration layer. The representative business services at Level 1, Level 2 and Level 3 are listed in Table 5.6. These business services are illustrative in nature.

5.3.4.7 Information Service

Enterprise information systems would expose its business entities as information services for accessing through portal, business processes, business services, integration and foundation services.

TABLE 5.5

Process Areas

#	Process Area	Process/subprocess
1	**Product Creation**	Product Strategy Product proposal and set up Authoring and development Production QA and Testing
2	**Market Execution**	Inventory receipt and management Order Mgmt. including customer information Order fulfillment and returns Non-physical access control Invoicing and Accounts Receivable Customer care Customer acquisition and retention
	Business Support	Vendor management and purchasing Accounts Payable Inventory Cost Accounting Royalties Management Revenue Recognition Financial Reporting Planning and Analysis Data reporting Treasury Management Rights and Licensing

TABLE 5.6

Business Services

Level 1	Level 2	Level 3
Content Management	Content Repository and Archival	Archival Library Services Storage
	Content Strategy	Content Sourcing Strategy Market Research
	Content Transformation	Format Transformation Standards Transformation
	Metadata Management	Content Tagging Metadata Schema Definition Taxonomy
	Search & Discovery	Contextual Search Faceted Search Image—Match Search Parametric Search Search Engine Optimization (SEO)

(Continued)

TABLE 5.6

(Continued)

Level 1	Level 2	Level 3
Customer Relationship Management	Customer Care	Case Management Customer Feedbacks & Surveys Multi-Channel Customer Interactions Self-Service Service Level Management
	Customer Data Management	Account / Contract Maintenance Customer Data Maintenance
	Customer Intelligence	Audience Segmentation Customer Analytics Customer Product Usage Tracking
	Customer Retention & Loyalty	Renewal Lead Generation Performance Tracking & Analytics Program Execution & Refinement Program Plan & Design
	Sales Management	3rd Party Sales Channel Integration Channel Management Contact Management Pipeline Management & Forecasting Proposal/Offer Management Prospecting & Qualification Sales Compensation Sales Reporting & Tracking
Financial Management	Accounting	Accruals and Adjustments Cash Reconciliation GL Account Reconciliation Operational Audits Inventory Accounting Regulatory Accounting
	Accounts Payable	Payables Management Purchase Order Processing
	Accounts Receivable	Credit and Collections Invoice Processing Receivables Management
	Asset Management	Capital Investment Analysis Facilities
	Corporate Finance	Cash Flow Management Compensation Design Employee Expense Reimbursement Financial Controls GL Maintenance Project/Job Costing Tax Treasury and Foreign Exchange
	Planning & Analysis	Budget Control Structure Policies and Procedures Pricing and Profitability Management Reporting Strategic Planning
	Regulatory & Financial Reporting	External Internal Managerial

Level 1	Level 2	Level 3
Marketing Management	Branding and Corporate Communication	Brand Management Corporate Communications
	Product Marketing and Campaign Management	Marketing Lead Generation Marketing/Campaign Plan & Design Marketing/Campaign Execution & Refinement Performance Tracking & Analytics
Order Management	Inventory Management	Forecasting Inventory Planning & Management Obsolescence Management Physical/Cycle Counting Replenishment
	Order Fulfillment &Invoicing	3rd Party Fulfillment Channel Integration Distribution (Digital) Invoicing Access Management
	Order Processing	3rd Party Order Channel Integration Order Entry & Validation Order Maintenance Order Tracking Subscription Renewal Tokens Management
	Returns Processing	Authorize Return Disposition Return Financial Settlement Receive & Adjust Inventory Returns Validation
	Physical Distribution Management	Receiving Putaway Pick Pack Ship Transportation Replenishment
Procurement and Vendor Management	Partner/Vendor Performance Management	Benchmarking Ongoing Contract Management Measurement Risk Mitigation
	Procurement	PO creation PO tracking Workflow
	Spend Analytics	Analysis Classification codes Sourcing plans
	Vendor Selection	Contract Negotiation-Signing Rev erse auctions RFI/RFP Vendor analysis

(Continued)

TABLE 5.6

(Continued)

Level 1	Level 2	Level 3
Product Management	Product Intelligence	Global/Regional Product Usage Tracking Market Segmentation Product Analytics
	Product Performance Management	Product Cost Reporting Product Lifecycle Analysis Product Profitability Analysis Product Revenue reporting
	Product Portfolio Mgt.	Product Line Strategy Management Product Line Comparison
	Product R&D	Pricing Management Product/service Catalog Management
	Product Strategy	Product Definition Product Lifecycle Management Sourcing/Partnership Management Permissions definition Permissions negotiation
Pricing and Discounts	Pricing Management	Price Models Price Negotiation Price Workflow
	Discounts Management	Discount Models Discount Workflow

Representative list of enterprise information services or systems are as follows:

- Customer
- Product
- Partner/Vendor
- Content
- Content Metadata
- Permissions
- Licenses
- Order
- CRM
- Sales
- HR
- Finance
- Legal
- Sales/Marketing
- Reporting
- Analytics

5.3.4.8 Integration Layer

The integration layer will provide services to integrate application services, data services, internal enterprise applications, and external services like partner, vendor. It comprises of enterprise messaging service, adapter services and legacy integration services that integrate disparate services, components and enterprise applications. The integration can be either asynchronous or synchronous depending on the nature of application. It uses various adapters that include FTP, SOAP, XML, JMS and DB for integrating the services running on even different platforms.

Responsible for providing mediation and transformation through common integration services to enable integration agility. It acts as an integration backbone for internal system interactions as well as external system interactions.

Representative list of services supported by the layer are listed in Table 5.7

Presentation layer, Business process layer, foundation services, data services will be communicating each other via this integration backbone. This enables loose coupling and promotes reuse and standard way of interfacing and helps minimize point to point integration issues.

5.3.4.9 Foundation Layer

Foundation Layer represents enterprise common standards, frameworks, technology reusable services, matured foundation platforms that need to be enforced at enterprise level to align with Architecture Principles. It also encompasses platforms services that provide development and runtime platform and/or span across multiple LOBs.

The foundation services often undergo an evolution path through steps as outlined here: standards definition to frameworks evaluation, extension of frameworks as reusable services, centralization of services with development and runtime platform, etc. In general, the approach is determined by the organization's IT maturity and requirements of each foundation service.

TABLE 5.7

Integration Layer Services

Service Name	Description
Application Adapter	Adapter services to integrate with applications like SAP, Oracle, Siebel, PeopleSoft, J.D. Edwards
Protocol Adapter	Support of various communication protocols like HTTP, FTP, web services like SOAP & REST, Messaging like MQ & JMS
Routing	Capability to have addressability, static/deterministic routing, content-based routing, rules-based routing, policy-based routing
Transformation	Service for message-processing, message transformation and message enhancement
Aggregation	Capability to perform coordination of multiple implementation services exposed as a single aggregated service
Legacy Integration	Legacy integration services
Mediation	Capability to perform protocol transformation and service mapping in synchronous and asynchronous pattern

The foundation services layer comprises of:

- Frameworks: Includes common standards and framework libraries (e.g. Struts, Spring MVC, Webwork) to enforce standardization and accelerate productivity.
- Technology Services: Includes common standards, framework libraries and reusable services (e.g. Exception Management, UI Frameworks, Application Frameworks).
- Foundation Platforms: Includes centralized development and runtime platform (e.g. reporting, business analytics, web analytics, email services, enterprise search, security).

5.3.4.10 Frameworks

Table 5.8 notes some industry available solution options for the Foundation Frameworks ABB in alignment with the **Prefer Use over Buy over Build** Principle:

5.3.4.11 Technology Services

Technology Services are those Foundation Layer ABBs which have callable service interface (Distributed or Centralized) that help to enforce standardization, architecture best practices, adopt design patterns and consistent programming at enterprise level.

Technology Services typically have following characteristics:

- Common technical capability that can be reused at enterprise or LOB level
- Business agnostic
- Maximum potential for reuse
- Either reusable libraries as a service or hosted as centralized service
- Standard interface specifications and usage guidelines
- Adopts best of breed architecture and design patterns

TABLE 5.8

Foundation Layer Services

Service Name	Description
Cache Frameworks	Standard framework for caching requirements (e.g. OSCache, EHCache)
Logging Frameworks	Standard framework for Logging/Auditing like Log4j, JMS implementation
Business Rules Frameworks	Standard framework for BRMS like Drools, Blaze
Workflow Frameworks	Standard framework implementing workflow capability (e.g. jBPM)
UI Framework/s	Standard framework for user interface like Adobe Flex, GWT, JSF, Spring MVC
Application Framework/s	Standard framework for business logic like Spring.Java, Spring.net
Web 2.0 Frameworks	Standard frameworks for achieving Web 2.0 features like RIA framework, AJAX, Flex
ORM Framework	Standard framework for Object Relational Mapping like Hibernate, myBATIS
Mobile Frameworks	Standard framework for implementing mobile services

- Can be realized through:
  - o Out-of-the-box frameworks (or) product capability
  - o Out-of-the-box frameworks/products extended for enterprise requirements
  - o Custom built services
- Considerations:
  - o Each building block can have one or more implementable services
  - o Realization can be through product out-of-the-box feature, open source framework/s or custom build (listed in the order of preference)
  - o Custom builds have to be justified with specific requirements to adhere with EA principle
  - o Expected to grow based on the continuous needs of reusability among the enterprise applications

Table 5.9 provides a set of potential technology services based on reuse potential seen across industries.

TABLE 5.9

Technology Services

Service Name	Description
Logging & Auditing	Enterprise Logging Service with set of service interfaces for other consumers to accomplish their logging and auditing functionality with centralized runtime platform
BRMS (Rules Management)	Enterprise Rules Management Service with set of service interfaces for other consumers to accomplish their rules development, deployment and execution with centralized runtime platform
Document Management	Standard framework for managing the storing and retrieval of raw documents (e.g. Leverage SharePoint API and exposing it as service)
Exception Management	Enterprise Exception Management provides a set of service interfaces for consumers to accomplish their business exception and system exception with niche functionalities such as actionable alerts, workflow etc.
Workflow Management	Workflow Management service provides a set of service interfaces for consumers to accomplish their workflow functionalities
Notification Service	Common Notification Service that would be used for sending alerts, status notification, etc. through various medium such as Email, SMS and social networking platforms
Scheduler	Common service that provides runtime platform for on-demand scheduling, time-based scheduling and dependent schedules
Configuration	Common service that externalizes the configurable resources that include infrastructure related parameters, thresh holds etc. It works effectively with business rules engine for externalization
Cross Reference	Common service that provides data store and service interface for accommodating domain translation, primary key translation for master data
Visibility	Common service that tracks the process flow and alert the appropriate users for any actionable events

5.3.4.12 Foundation Platforms

Foundation Platforms are reusable functions which support the functionality of most of the architecture building blocks (Figure 5.6 and Table 5.10). These functions have potential opportunity for creating centralized development and runtime platform with reusable services that help to enforce standardization, architecture best practices, adopt design patterns and consistent programming.

Foundation Platform typically has following characteristics:

- Provides common business functionality that is required at enterprise/LOB level
- Provides centralized development and runtime platform
- Continuous support for the consumers of this shared services
- Exposes its common functionality as services to other systems
- Publishes standards and interface specifications for the development and runtime platform

5.3.4.13 External Integration

This layer represents Integration services which provide Enterprise applications to have a capability to communicate with external systems of partner, vendor, and analyst sources.

- Partner Integration: Integrating with partners such as Agencies, and Distributors for data interchange.
- Vendor Integration: Integrating with vendors in the areas of finished goods etc. for data interchange.
- External Services: Integrating with external service agencies for data such as Foreign Exchange, Payment Gateways, Credit cards, address validation and Banks.
- Content Integration Services: Integrating with external data provider agencies for data acquisition & content data delivery to other providers.

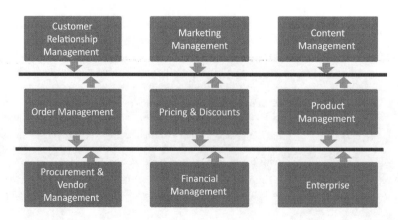

FIGURE 5.6
Foundation Platforms.

TABLE 5.10

Foundation Platform Services

Service Name	Description
Mobile Services	Mobile Enterprise application Platform with set of frameworks, standards, development platform and runtime infrastructure
IVR Services	IVR Enterprise application Platform with set of frameworks, standards, development platform and runtime infrastructure
FAX Services	FAX Integration Platform with set of frameworks, standards, integration specification and runtime infrastructure
Web 2.0	Enterprise Web 2.0 Platform with set of frameworks, standards, development platform and runtime infrastructure
Social Networking	Social Networking Platform with set of frameworks, standards, development platform and runtime infrastructure
Business Analytics	Enterprise platform and standard framework with development and runtime infrastructure to analyze the business events and generate reports
Business Activity Monitoring	Enterprise platform and standard framework with development and runtime infrastructure to capture the business events and analyze in real-time and send it to business analytical engine
Web Analytics	Enterprise platform and standard framework with development and runtime infrastructure to capture the user activity events and send it to analytical platform
Reporting	Enterprise platform and standard framework with development and runtime infrastructure to develop, execute and deliver all types of reports
Search	Enterprise platform and standard framework with development and runtime infrastructure to implement search on content, document, people
MDM Services	Enterprise Master Data Management (MDM) platform for development and execution of MDM data services
Security	Standard framework for implementing SSO, authentication, Authorization, digital security
Email Services	Enablement of Email Service that includes setup, maintain and support of exchange platform
Issue Management	Enablement of issue management Service that includes supporting tools and technologies of issue management
Managed File Transfer	Enterprise platform for centralized and automated file transfer management
Others	Other services which are envisaged in future or not covered here

5.3.5 Architectural Building Blocks: PIM

In this section, following ABBs are covered within context of future state enterprise architecture.

- Business functions (e.g. CRM, Order Management, etc.) are elaborated in detail from platform independent perspective accompanied with a brief description.
- Technology functions (e.g. Application container, portal) and Foundation Services (e.g. Frameworks, Technology Services, Platforms) are elaborated from platform independent perspective. For each the following sections are provided: overview, enabling technology capabilities, alignment with architecture principles and supporting business capabilities.

5.3.5.1 ABBs: Business Functions

In this section, each architecture building block that is associated with Business Service is elaborated.

Figure 5.7 shows the next level details of the business service layer of the future state enterprise architecture view with three levels of decomposition of the highest level business services.

5.3.5.1.1 Content Management

Figure 5.8 depicts the architecture building blocks of Content Management with brief description (Tables 5.11–5.15).

FIGURE 5.7
Architecture Building Blocks—Enterprise Business Functions.

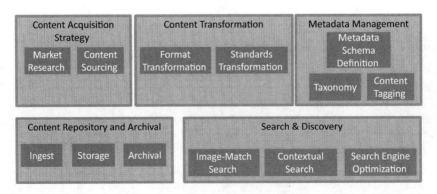

FIGURE 5.8
ABB—Content Management Business Functions.

TABLE 5.11

Content Acquisition Strategy

Content Acquisition Strategy	
Content Sourcing Strategy	Tools to identify sources of content for desired product
Market Research	Research on market needs for content Comparison of proposed content/product to similarly themed releases

TABLE 5.12

Content Transformation

Content Transformation	
Format Transformation	Tools to automate transformation of files from one format to another format
Standards Transformation	For XML documents, transformation of XML-based content from one standard to another standard

TABLE 5.13

Metadata Management

Metadata Management	
Content Tagging	Metadata tagging of content objects. Semantic tagging of content (inline tagging)
Metadata Schema Definition	Definition and updating of metadata model Updating of content to match changes to metadata model XML Schema: For XML documents only
Taxonomy	Hierarchical classification of content, normally based on codes stored as metadata

TABLE 5.14

Search & Discovery

Search & Discovery	
Contextual Search	Search for content files based on the data/content contained in the files
Faceted Search	Search based on assigning classifications to content objects, with each classification presented as a facet
Image—Match Search	Specific only to images; pixel-matching algorithms find matches to selected image
Parametric Search	Search based on metadata parameters
Search Engine Optimization (SEO)	Improving search engine discoverability of content

TABLE 5.15

Content Repository and Archival

Content Repository and Archival	
Archival	Collecting files in a centralized system; May include tools to move less frequently accessed files to near-line/offline storage
Ingestion	Tools to ingest content into CMS; May automate extraction of metadata
Library Services	Check-in/check-out services (allowing only one user to edit a file at one time) Versioning (creating and saving multiple versions of files as they go through an editing/production cycle)
Storage	Storage of files in a centralized system; obviously related to Archival

5.3.5.1.2 *CRM & Sales*

Figure 5.9 depicts the architecture building blocks of CRM with brief description (Table 5.16 –5.20).

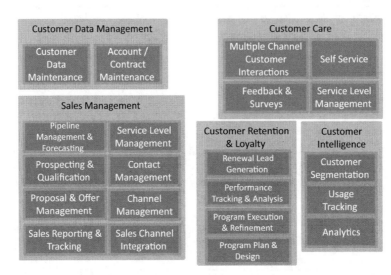

FIGURE 5.9
ABB—Customer Relationship Management Business functions.

TABLE 5.16

Customer Care

Customer Care	
Case Management	Management of "trouble tickets" from customers Taking trouble tickets Managing issues to resolution
Customer Feedbacks & Surveys	Feedback into customer care process from product/ service users, buyers Survey definition Survey execution
Multi-Channel Customer Interactions	Management of issues coming from multiple customer-facing sales or fulfillment channels
Self-Service	Portal-based methods to enable customers to enter customer care issues online
Service Level Management	Tracking of customer care against SLAs

TABLE 5.17

Customer Data Management

Customer Data Management	
Account/Contract Maintenance	Creation & Maintenance of customer account data Creation & Maintenance of customer contract data
Customer Data Maintenance	Gathering of data on customer interaction with organization Maintenance of customer data

TABLE 5.18

Customer Intelligence

Customer Intelligence	
Audience Segmentation	Use of customer data to divide customers into sub-groups to be targeted Gathering of demographic data Gathering of psychographic data
Customer Analytics	Gathering data on customer behavior with products/services
Customer Product Usage Tracking	Gathering of customers' product usage data Updating of customers' product usage data Accumulation of all usage data for specific products

TABLE 5.19

Customer Retention & Loyalty

Customer Retention & Loyalty	
Renewal Lead Generation	For existing customers with contracts/subscriptions about to expire, identification and generation of those leads
Performance Tracking & Analytics	Tracking of 'churn' rate (number of existing customers who continue to buy products) Analysis of products for which churn rate is high/low Analysis of customers segments to determine segment churn rates
Program Execution & Refinement	Retention/loyalty program execution Retention/loyalty program refinement
Program Plan & Design	Retention/loyalty program (marketing) definition

TABLE 5.20

Sales Management

Sales Management	
3rd Party Sales Channel Integration	Integration with non-organization sales channels
Channel Management	Identifying appropriate sales channels for specific products/services Managing individual sales channels Analysis of sales channel performance
Contact Management	Recording sales rep interaction with current/prospective customers Monitoring sales rep interaction with customers
Pipeline Management & Forecasting	Identification of likely purchasers/users of products/services Management of most likely purchasers Forecasting based on prospects in pipeline
Proposal/Offer Management	Creation of proposals for sales to, for example, STMS societies Delivery/communication of proposals Receipt of counter-proposals Management of proposals/offers made and accepted
Prospecting & Qualification	Prospecting for new sales opportunities Qualification of identified sales opportunities as valid leads
Sales Compensation	Calculation of compensation to be paid to sales reps Payment of compensation to sales reps
Sales Reporting & Tracking	Reporting of sales activity against targets Establishment of sales targets Tracking of sales performance against sales targets

5.3.5.1.3 Marketing Management

Figure 5.10 depicts the architecture building blocks of Marketing Management business function (Tables 5.20 and 5.22).

5.3.5.1.4 Product Management

Figure 5.11 depicts the architecture building blocks of Product Management with brief description (Tables 5.23–5.27).

FIGURE 5.10
ABB—Marketing Management Business Functions.

TABLE 5.21

Branding and Corporate Communications

Branding and Corporate Communications	
Brand Management	Management of overall brand
	Establishment of branding for individual BUs/imprints
	Management of branding for individual BUs/imprints
Corporate Communications	Communications issued internally (employees, shareholders)
	Communications issued to external bodies (channel partners, media, government., etc.)

TABLE 5.22

Product Marketing and Campaign Management

Product Marketing and Campaign Management	
Marketing Lead Generation	Campaigns to attract new customers
	Gathering of leads from marketing campaigns
Marketing/Campaign Plan & Design	Planning and design of marketing campaigns
Marketing/Campaign Execution & Refinement	Execution of marketing campaigns
	Ongoing updating and refinement of marketing campaigns
Performance Tracking & Analytics	Tracking of marketing campaign performance

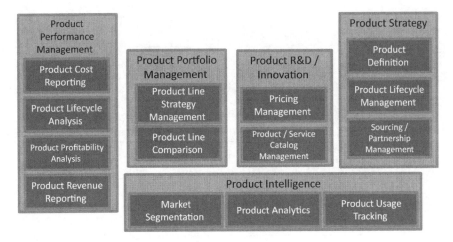

FIGURE 5.11
ABB—Product Management Business Functions.

TABLE 5.23

Product Intelligence

Product Intelligence	
Global/Regional Product Usage Tracking	Tracking of product usage across regions Tracking of product usage globally Tracking of usage of individual products
Market Segmentation	Use of customer and product data to define markets to be targeted
Product Analytics	Analytics of proposed products against performance of comparable products in marketplace

TABLE 5.24

Product Performance Management

Product Performance Management	
Product Cost Reporting	Tracking and analysis of product cost data (unit costs, production costs, distribution costs, etc.)
Product Lifecycle Analysis	Analysis of product viability to establish its renewal or obsolescence
Product Profitability Analysis	Analysis of product profitability
Product Revenue reporting	Reporting of revenue for individual products Reporting of revenue for product lines (rollup to chemistry, accounting, etc.) Rollup of revenue reporting to BU, global levels

TABLE 5.25

Product Portfolio Management

Product Portfolio Management	
Product Line Strategy Management	Development and management of strategies for product lines (within current BUs and across BUs)
Product Line Comparison	Analytics of entire product line against performance of comparable product lines in marketplace

TABLE 5.26

Product R&D

Product R&D	
Pricing Management	For new products, analysis of pricing of comparable products For existing products, analysis of changes to comparable product pricing Establishment and management of product pricing
Product/Service Catalog Management	Management of product information in structured manner

TABLE 5.27

Product Strategy

Product Strategy	
Product Definition	Definition of content, product or service to meet perceived marketplace need
Product Lifecycle Management	Management of products from conception, through design and manufacture, through updates, to obsolescence
Sourcing/Partnership Management	Management of vendors or partners involved in the development of content and/or product

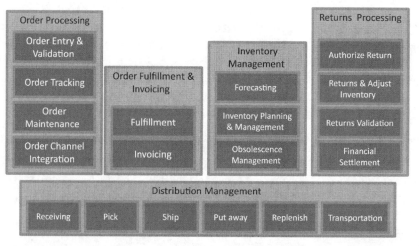

FIGURE 5.12
ABB—Order Management Business Functions.

5.3.5.1.5 Order Management

Figure 5.12 depicts the architecture building blocks of Order Management with brief description (Tables 5.28–5.32).

5.3.5.1.6 Pricing and Discounts

Figure 5.13 depicts the architecture building blocks of Price and Discounts Management with brief description (Table 5.33).

TABLE 5.28

Order Processing

Order Processing	
3rd Party Order Channel Integration	Integration of 3rd parties and 3rd party systems used by intermediaries to sell product
Order Entry & Validation	Entry of orders for intermediaries taken through sales on internal systems Entry of order made by direct customers taken through online portal Validation that data elements of order are correct, do not break business rules
Order Maintenance	Maintenance of incoming orders
Order Tracking	Tracking status of order, from order entry through fulfillment
Subscription Renewal	Functions to manage renewal of subscription products Functions to 'tickle' internal users when customer subscriptions are about to expire Functions to 'tickle' external users when their subscriptions are about to expire
Tokens Management	Managing the tokens that are used to provide access to online content as part of order fulfillment

TABLE 5.29

Order Fulfillment & Invoicing

Order Fulfillment & Invoicing	
3rd Party Fulfillment Channel Integration	Integration of 3rd parties and 3rd party systems used by intermediaries to distribute product
Distribution	Distribution of product—covers both fulfillment scenario as well as supplying to a vendor
Invoicing	Invoicing of intermediaries (wholesale) Invoicing of direct customers (retail) Pricing for invoicing
Access Management	Managing Digital access

TABLE 5.30

Inventory Management

Inventory Management	
Forecasting	Estimating the quantity of products that intermediaries and/or direct customers will purchase
Inventory Planning& Management	Planning amount of inventory needed, accommodating cycles of greater or lesser demand
Obsolescence Management	Tracking of when current inventory of time-sensitive product will become obsolete. Management of cross-over between 'old' (obsolete) inventory and new
Physical/Cycle Counting	Physical: Facility operation stops, all inventory on hand counted Cycle: Small subsets of inventory counted; cycle continues until entire inventory counted

TABLE 5.31

Physical Distribution Management

Physical Distribution Management	
Receiving	Reception of physical product at warehouse
Putaway	After reception of goods at warehouse, placing inventory on shelves/in storage
Pick	Picking inventory to be shipped
Pack	Packing inventory for shipment
Ship	Shipment of orders Tracking of order shipments
Transportation	Consists of shipping costs and other configuration details related to transportation
Replenishment	Replenishment of inventory

TABLE 5.32

Returns Processing

Returns Processing	
Authorize Return	Returns must be authorized by (some products may not be returned)
Disposition Return	Decision on what to do with returned inventory
Financial Settlement	For either intermediaries or direct customers, reimbursement of monies spent and adjustment of financial statements
Receive & Adjust Inventory	If products are re-sellable, they are re-combined with remaining inventory, and inventory counts adjusted
Returns Validation	Validation of returned products before adjusting the credit

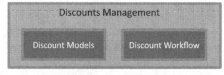

FIGURE 5.13
ABB—Price and Discounts Management Business Functions.

TABLE 5.33

Pricing and Discounts

Pricing and Discounts	
Pricing Models	Comprises of various price model definitions and its functionality
Price Workflow	Workflows that are needed for flexible pricing
Price Negotiation	Functionality to handle customer price negotiations
Discount Models	Discount Model definitions and its functional logic
Discount Workflow	Workflows that are needed for Flexible promotions

5.3.5.1.7 Rights and Royalties

Figure 5.14 depicts the architecture building blocks of Rights and Royalties with brief description (Tables 5.34–5.36).

FIGURE 5.14
Rights and Royalties Business Functions.

TABLE 5.34

Rights Management

Rights Management	
Content rights definition	Definition of rights
Rights compliance tracking	Tracking of compliance with terms of rights agreements
Rights renewal	When rights have expired, negotiation of rights extension
Content rights negotiation	Negotiation of licensing terms with potential 3rd parties

TABLE 5.35

Royalty Management

Royalty Management	
Advance calculation	If contract specifies advance, calculation of that advance, and adjustment of future payments because of advance
Royalty contract management	Creation of royalty contracts Management of royalty contracts (renewal/re-negotiation, etc.)
Royalty payment calculation	Calculation of royalty payment due

TABLE 5.36

Permissions Management

Permissions Management	
Permissions compliance tracking	Tracking of 3rd party compliance with terms of licensing agreements
Permissions definition	Definition of licensing opportunity to be offered to 3rd parties
Permissions negotiation	Negotiation of licensing terms with potential 3rd parties Selection of 3rd party for licensing opportunity

5.3.5.1.8 Procurement and Vendor Management

Figure 5.15 depicts the architecture building blocks of Procurement and Vendor Management with brief description (Tables 5.37–5.39).

5.3.5.1.9 Financial Management

Figure 5.16 depicts the architecture building blocks of Financial Management with brief description (Tables 5.40–5.46).

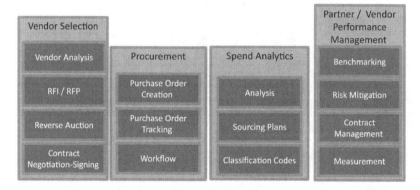

FIGURE 5.15
ABB—Procurement and Vendor Management Business Functions.

TABLE 5.37

Vendor Selection and Procurement

Vendor Selection	
Contract Negotiation-Signing	Negotiation of contract terms with "short list"/final vendor Signing and management of contract with final vendor selection
Reverse auctions	Management of process whereby vendors compete over service bid
RFs	Development, distribution and response management of RFIs, RFPs, etc.
Vendor analysis	Analysis of appropriate vendors (existing and new) to meet business requirement
Procurement	
PO creation	Creation of purchase orders for procurement
PO tracking	Tracking of purchase orders for procurement
Workflow	Monitoring of procurement from purchase order creation through accounts payable process

TABLE 5.38

Partner/Vendor Performance Management

Partner/Vendor Performance Management	
Benchmarking	Establishment of standards for partner/vendor performance
Ongoing Contract Management	Management of contracts with partners/vendors, with updates to contracts as necessary
Measurement	Evaluation of partner/vendor performance against established benchmarks
Risk Mitigation	Development of plans for replacement of vendors if performance/company viability suffers

TABLE 5.39

Spend Analytics

Spend Analytics	
Analysis	Analysis of procurement/spending across the enterprise
Classification codes	Use of material codes to track spends of commodity items
Sourcing plans	Planning for sourcing of commodity spending

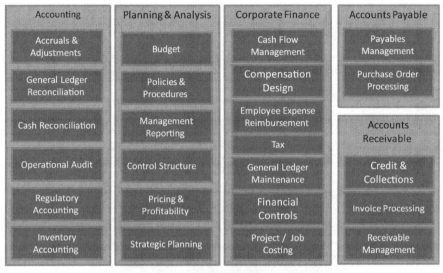

FIGURE 5.16
ABB—Financial Management Business Functions.

TABLE 5.40

Accounting

Accounting	
Accruals and Adjustments	Revenue or expenses earned or incurred which are not yet recorded
Cash Reconciliation	Management of cash which is synchronized to bank balances
GL Account Reconciliation	Resolution of account discrepancies across regions, products, etc.
Operational Audits	Evaluation of performance and conformity to policy
Regulatory Accounting	Compliance with certain rules and regulations of accounting
Inventory Accounting	Cost accounting of inventory

TABLE 5.41

Accounts Payable

Accounts Payable	
Payables Management	Administration of a company's debts or liabilities
Purchase Order Processing	Execution of the purchase order and reconciliation process in purchasing

TABLE 5.42

Accounts Receivable

Accounts Receivable	
Credit and Collections	Credit Management, Assignment of lines of credit and collection of payments
Invoice Processing	Handling of incoming invoices from arrival to post
Receivables Management	Administration of a company's costs of goods and services sold

TABLE 5.43

Asset Management

Asset Management	
Capital Investment Analysis	Assessment of capital usage
Facilities	Assessment of capital specific to facilities and their operations

TABLE 5.44

Regulatory & Financial Reporting

Regulatory & Financial Reporting	
External	Financial reporting for use outside of a company to report on planned and actual results
Internal	Financial reporting for use within company to measure effectiveness and efficiency of operations
Managerial	Broad category of reporting and analytics to assist in decision making

TABLE 5.45

Corporate Finance

Corporate Finance	
Cash Flow Management	Monitoring, analyzing and adjusting business cash flow between inflows and outflows
Compensation Design	Creation of compensation and incentive structures
Employee Expense Reimb	Management of employee business expenses
Financial Controls	Financial processes to help organization accomplish financial management
GL Maintenance	Ongoing design of GL structure and accounts
Project/Job Costing	Management and allocation of resource costs to specific programs
Tax	Planning and execution of tax payments and Country/State Tax management
Treasury and ForEx	Management of company's currencies

TABLE 5.46

Planning & Analysis

Planning & Analysis	
Budget	Setting of initial revenue and cost projections
Control Structure	Design of processes to help organization accomplish its goals
Policies and Procedures	Structured guidelines for financial operations
Pricing and Profitability	Analysis of product and geographic income potential
Management Reporting	Broad category of reporting and analytics to assist in decision making
Strategic Planning	Long-term planning taking into account market, competitor and customer movements

5.3.6 ABBs: Technology Functions

In this section, each architecture building block that is associated with Technology functions is elaborated from Platform Independent perspective. They are broadly reviewed for the following aspects:

- Overview: Definition of building block
- Need: Value proposition of having this building block
- Enabling Technology Capabilities: key features or requirements that would help the solution to strive toward the business capabilities and Architecture Principles
- Traceability: provides the drivers:
  - o Architecture Principles
  - o Business Capability
  - o Architectural Observations

    Technology functions are broadly classified into:
- Web containers: to provide base platform for presentation services
- Application containers: to provide base platform for business services
- Portal: helps to realize presentation layer
- BPM: helps to realize process orchestration layer
- Integration platform: helps to realize integration layer

5.3.7 Web Container

Web Container refers to the Architecture Building Block responsible for providing deployment platform to execute web components of portal services in the overall envisioned enterprise architecture.

Table 5.47 describes the Web Container characteristics.

TABLE 5.47

Web Container Characteristics

Overview	Web Server is software framework that provides an environment where web application run and delivers web pages over intranet and/or internet
Need	Web Container Standardization is needed to enable:
	• Technology Standardization • Adopting to emerging technology in the Web container arena
Enabling Technology Capabilities	**Enabling Technology Capabilities** to be considered for Web Server rationalization includes the following:
	• Security (basic, digest, SSL) • OpenSSL support for faster performance • Virtual hosting • IPV6 support • HTTP, HTTPS, FTP, FTPS, SMTP SUPPORT • Software load balancing (Application Request Routing) • Single Sign On (SSO) Support • Caching, compression • Clustering, and high availability • Administration console • Role-based interface • Servlet support (only for Java Web Server) • Cross-OS platform • WebDAV support • Multiple web platform support (e.g. PHP, Servlet, JSP, CGI)
Traceability	
Principles	Following Architecture Principles to be adhered during Web Server selection process:
	• **Prefer Use over Buy over Build** • **Avoid Current State Driving/Constraining Future State Design** • **Delineate Architectural Responsibility** • **Base Architecture on Service Orientation** • **Comply to Standards** • **Rationalize Technology**
Business Capability	Web Container supports indirectly either partially or fully enabling the following business capabilities:
	• Enterprise Technology Planning and Cost-effective Operation (e.g. Web Server Selection)
Architectural Observations	The following observation has identified the Web Server rationalization and Unified Portal Platform solution:
	• Need for enterprise-wide Web Server Standardization and Rationalization

5.3.8 Application Container

Application Container refers to the architecture building block responsible for providing deployment platform to execute portal, process orchestration, business services, and integration and information services in the overall envisioned enterprise architecture.

TABLE 5.48

Application Container Characteristics

Overview	Application Server is software framework that provides an environment where applications can run and acts as a set of components accessible for software development through an API defined by the selected platform itself
Need	Application Container Standardization is needed to enable: • Technology Standardization • Adopting to emerging technology in the Application container arena
Enabling Technology Capabilities	**Enabling Technology Capabilities** to be considered for application server rationalization includes the following: • JEE/.NET Standards and Technologies support (e.g. JTA, StAX,.NET framework) • Web Container and Java Bean Support • Interoperability with frameworks such as Spring.Net, Spring.Java, ORM etc. • Administration Console • Caching, Clustering, High Availability • Security (Pluggable authentication, SSO, Message channel security, etc.) • Cloud-friendly
Traceability	
Principles	Following Architecture Principles to be adhered during Application Server selection process: • **Prefer Use over Buy over Build** • **Avoid Current State Driving/Constraining Future State Design** • **Delineate Architectural Responsibility** • **Base Architecture on Service Orientation** • **Comply to Standards** • **Rationalize Technology**
Business Capability	Application Container supports indirectly either partially or fully in enabling the following business capabilities. • Enterprise Technology Planning and Cost-effective Operation (e.g. Application Server Selection)
Architectural Observations	The following observation has identified the Portal Platform rationalization and Unified Portal Platform solution. • Need for Enterprise-wide Application Server Standardization and Rationalization

Table 5.48 describes the Application Container characteristics.

5.3.9 Portal/Presentation

Portal is the Architecture Building Block responsible for managing the presentation logic and its views in the overall envisioned enterprise architecture.

Table 5.49 describes the portal platform characteristics from PIM perspective.

As part of portal, eCommerce is also one of the key functionalities that help enterprise to provide base platform for selling of their products electronically (Table 5.50).

TABLE 5.49

Portal Platform Characteristics

Overview	Portal/s is the one of the web channels that would be considered as single point of entry for all the/external users and partners and vendors to interact with organization system using browsers. Portal comprises of all the user interfaces that encompasses both vertical (to name a few: CRM, Order Processing, Finance etc.) and horizontal portal functionalities (such as administration portals etc.)
Need	Portal layer and Unified portal platform is needed to enable: • Consistent user experience • UI Portal Technology Standardization • Faster Development • Adopting to emerging technology in the portal space • Improved separation of concerns
Enabling Technology Capabilities	Portal platform needs to have key IT enablers for enabling business capabilities to achieve strategic objectives that includes the following: • RICH Internet Experience Capability (Web 2.0 support) • Content Collaboration and Unification • Internationalization & Localization • Personalization: Role-based User experience servicing B2E, B2C, B2B (Internal Users, External Users, Agents, Partner/Vendor etc.) • Enterprise Mash-ups & Dashboards • Social Networking (wiki, RSS, blogs, polls, alerts etc.) • Web Oriented Architecture (WOA) • Web Service support (RESTFul, Portlets) • Cloud Friendly • Standards Support (WS-*, Portlets)
Traceability	
Principles	The Portal Platform should be identified in alignment with the following Architecture Principles. Starting from portal strategy to implementation, the following Principles need to be adhered to • **Prefer Use over Buy over Build** • **Set Up Enterprise Solutions with Local Variants** • **Drive for Reusable Solution Building Blocks** • **Avoid Current State Driving/Constraining Future State Design** • **Delineate Architectural Responsibility** • **Base Architecture on Service Orientation** • **Comply to Standards** • **Rationalize Technology**
Business Capability	Rationalization of the Vertical Portals and Horizontal Portals with a unified portal solution works toward enabling the following business capabilities: • Enterprise Customer Care (e.g. Customer Care Portal) • 360 Degree Enterprise Customer View (e.g. CRM Portal, Customer Care Portal) • Enterprise Technology Planning and Cost-effective Operation (e.g. Portal Selection, Framework development) • Product Localization (e.g. Portal Personalization based on Product, Geography, roles, business unit)
Architectural Observations	The following observation is relevant for the Portal Platform rationalization and Unified Portal Platform solution. • Need for Enterprise-wide Portal Platform rationalization for each domain

TABLE 5.50

eCommerce Functionality

Overview	eCommerce is commonly referred as buying and selling of products electronically to consumers or other partners. In this context, it is a shared service as part of portal platform that would serve all eCommerce functionalities

Enabling Technology Capabilities	• Direct to Customer
	   • Search/Browse products, rich shopping cart with personalization, product comparison, promotions, multi-channel order entry, self-service, cross-sells
	• Integration
	   • Integration with backend systems such as ERP, Content management, customer care and CRM, finance and BI systems.
	   • Integration with analytics products (e.g. Google Analytics).
	• Product and WCM (Web Content Management)
	   • Supporting editorial, vendor supplied, syndicated and user-generated
	   • WCM—Addressing SEO and multi-channels
	   • Marketing and Promotion Tools

5.3.10 Enterprise Integration Platform

This refers to the Architecture Building Block responsible for managing the common technical functions needed during integration of application to application with any to any data formats using varied protocols.

Table 5.51 describes the Enterprise Integration platform characteristics.

TABLE 5.51

Enterprise Integration Platform Characteristics

Overview	Enterprise integration platform is a common mediation layer that would serve as intermediary for all internal and external application (or) System interactions. Enterprise Integration platform relates to the Integration Layer in the Enterprise Architecture. This addresses the requirements and concerns associated with application and data integration.
Need	Integration layer and enterprise integration platform is needed to enable: • Integration Technology Standardization • Faster Integration Services Development • Adopting to emerging technology in the integration space • Leading to improved separation of concerns between user, application, partner and content integration • Common canonical used to transfer data • Reusable integration services (e.g. Order Management from/to Finance, CMS from/to Product Management) • Improving integration agility by avoiding point to point communication • Providing common gateway for external communications (Partner, Vendor, Content Providers and Consumers, Sales Channels, External Service Integration and so on) with IT Systems

(continued)

TABLE 5.51

(Continued)

Enabling Technology Capabilities	Enterprise Integration platform needs to have key IT enablers for enabling business capabilities that includes: • Support for multiple protocols and message formats connectivity • Support for multiple web services stack • Pre-built Adapter Support for protocol, packaged and legacy applications • Custom Adapter development support • Standard Compliance (XML and Web Services etc.) • Security—Authentication & Authorization framework • Application Server Support (J2EE Container support) • High Availability and scalability • Messaging backbone Support (e.g. JMS, MQ)
Traceability	
Principles	The following set of Architecture Principles needs to be enforced from the ESB platform selection through strategy to implementation: • **Prefer Use over Buy over Build** • **Drive for Reusable Solution Building Blocks** • **Avoid Current State Driving/Constraining Future State Design** • **Delineate Architectural Responsibility** • **Base Architecture on Service Orientation** • **Comply to Standards** • **Rationalize Technology** • **Secure Information** • **Reduce Manual Interventions**
Business Capability	The Enterprise Integration Platform with common ESB solution as part of Integration Layer is defined to contribute toward the following business capabilities: • Enterprise Customer Care (e.g. Integration of Customer Care with Back office systems) • 360 Degree Enterprise Customer View (e.g. Integration of CRM, CDM and Customer Care) • Enterprise approach to partner piloting, implementation and integration (e.g. Partner integration) • Enterprise Content and Service Bundling (e.g. Back office integration) • Enterprise Technology Planning and Cost-effective Operation (e.g. ESB Selection)
Architectural Observations	The following observation has identified the Integration/ESB Platform solution: • Common Enterprise-wide Integration Platform • Enterprise Application Integration Services based on Standard Interface contracts • Open Standard Technology Adoption • Emerging Technology Adoption • Integration Governance: Data access between enterprise systems may have to go through governance process

5.3.11 BPM

Process Management is the Architecture Building Block responsible for managing the process orchestrations with integration of portal, business, and integration functions in the enterprise architecture.

Table 5.52 describes the BPM platform helping to implement the process orchestration layer and its characteristics.

TABLE 5.52

BPM Platform Characteristics

Overview	BPM platform is the solution that provides the execution base for business processes to run on. It acts as an orchestration engine that controls the execution path of business process. BPM plays a role as part of Process Orchestration Layer in the Enterprise Architecture to address requirements and concerns associated with business process modeling, execution and integration
Need	Process Orchestration layer with BPM platform is needed to enable: • Agility in business process changes that arise due to market demand • Automated task execution to speed up the process execution time • Seamless Integration with heterogeneous application during business process execution lifecycle • Faster Processing time by reducing manual intervention • Flexible business processes through comprehensive support of process model features • Adopting to emerging technology in the BPM space • Improved separation of concerns between presentation and business services • Reusable process/sub-process services (e.g. Tax calculation, Price Calculation)
Enabling Technology Capabilities	BPM (Process Orchestration) platform needs to have the following key IT enablers (but not limited to) thus enabling business capabilities to achieve strategic objectives: • Comprehensive User interface for Process Modeling • Comprehensive Workflow including pre-built, custom workflow definition • Adhoc, dynamic workflows • Human-workflow management • Form and Document Supported workflow • Event-based • Integration with middleware technologies, Rules Engine, User store and Portal • Rich User Interface support for process life cycle execution • Process and Task administration • Standards compliance (BPMN 2.0, BPEL etc.) • Unified Eclipse-based design tool • Service Repository Integration
Traceability	
Principles	The following set of Architecture Principles needs to be enforced from the BPM platform selection through strategy to implementation: • **Prefer Use over Buy over Build** • **Drive for Reusable Solution Building Blocks** • **Avoid Current State Driving/Constraining Future State Design** • **Delineate Architectural Responsibility** • **Base Architecture on Service Orientation** • **Comply to Standards** • **Rationalize Technology** • **Reduce Manual Interventions**

(Continued)

TABLE 5.52

(Continued)

Business Capability	The BPM Platform as part of Process Orchestration Layer is defined to contribute toward the following business capabilities:

- Dynamic Content Management (e.g. Product Setup, Authoring, Production etc.)
- Product Localization (e.g. Product Setup, Authoring, Production etc.)
- Flexible Pricing and Quoting (e.g. Order Management Process, Invoicing and AR)
- Enterprise Customer Care (e.g. Customer Care)
- 360 Degree Enterprise Customer View (e.g. Customer Acquisition and Retention)
- Enterprise approach to partner piloting, implementation and integration (e.g. Customer Acquisition and Retention)
- Enterprise Content and Service Bundling (e.g. Order Management, Fulfillment etc.)
- Enterprise Technology Planning and Cost-effective Operation (e.g. BPM Selection)

Architectural Observations	The following observation has identified the Process Orchestration with BPM Platform solution:

- Rigid business processes that inhibit flexibility
- Absence of process orchestration using latest technology
- Open Standard Technology Adoption
- Emerging Technology Adoption

5.3.12 ABBs: Foundation

Foundational ABBs are responsible for providing base frameworks, reusable and centralized development and runtime platforms with standards and guidelines. In the enterprise architecture view, these are categorized as (Figure 5.17):

- Foundation Frameworks
- Technology Services
- Foundation Platforms

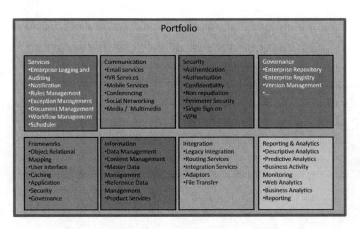

FIGURE 5.17
Foundation Services Categorization.

5.3.13 UI Framework

Table 5.53 describes the user interface framework foundation service overview and its importance.

TABLE 5.53

User Interface Framework

Overview	UI Framework/s are standard reusable libraries that accelerate user interface development by providing pre-built MVC handlers, exception management, validators, internationalization support and more. UI Framework is defined as part of foundation services in the Enterprise Architecture to address common set of UI framework standards & guidelines, reusable implementation UI framework. UI Frameworks can evolve as follows: • Define UI framework standards & guidelines that include criteria for usage of frameworks, list of Open Standard UI framework/s • Extend the open standard UI framework based on User Interface technical requirements and create reusable libraries for the applications to reuse in their architecture
Need	UI Framework/s are needed to: • Avoid multiple UI framework custom/open standard solutions being built or used • Adopt emerging technology in UI layer to support futuristic requirements • Improved separation of concerns between application User Interface and business process or business service layer • Reusable UI framework services • UI Framework Technology Standardization
Enabling Technology Capabilities	Enterprise UI Framework platform needs to have the following key IT enablers (and potentially others) thus enabling business capabilities to achieve strategic objectives: • Rapid Development—Library Support & IDE Support • Internationalization Support • Cross Browser/Platform Compatibility • MVC Architecture • Dependency Injection • Validation and Exception Handlers Support • Bookmark-ability & REST Support • Back button & Resubmit • AJAX Support • Tag Libraries • Support for multiple view technologies (e.g. JSP, Velocity, Tiles, iText, and POI)
Traceability	
Principles	The following set of Architecture Principles need to be enforced while, the UI framework/s are selected. • **Prefer Use over Buy over Build** • **Drive for Reusable Solution Building Blocks** • **Base Architecture on Service Orientation** • **Comply to Standards** • **Rationalize Technology**

(Continued)

TABLE 5.53

(Continued)

Business Capability	The Enterprise UI framework/s is defined to contribute toward the following business capabilities. • Enterprise Customer Care • Product Localization (e.g. User interface based on product selected and geography) • Enterprise Technology Planning and Cost-effective Operation (e.g. Logging and Auditing Framework Selection)
Architectural Observations	The following observation has identified the need for the User Interface framework/s solution: • Technology standardization • Emerging technology adoption

5.3.14 Application Framework

Table 5.54 describes the application framework/s foundation service overview and its importance.

TABLE 5.54

Application Framework/s

Overview	Enterprise application framework/s are set of standard libraries that accelerate business/application service development by providing pre-built Service invokers, validators, dependency injection, configurable xml loaders, annotation-based programming and more. Enterprise application framework/s is defined as part of foundation services in the Enterprise Architecture to address common set of Application framework standards & guidelines and reusable implementation application framework/s. Based on the level of maturity adoption, application framework/s can evolve as described below: • Define Application framework standards & guidelines, Open Standard Application framework/s catalog • Extend the open standard framework/s based on Business Service/Application Service Layer requirements and create extended application framework libraries for the enterprise applications to reuse in their architecture
Need	Enterprise application framework/s are needed to: • Avoid multiple custom application framework solutions being built • Avoid multiple open standard application framework/s being used • Enable Standardization of Business Service/Application Service Development • Adopt emerging technology in the business service/application service layer to address futuristic requirements • Improved separation of concerns between Portal/presentation layer and business service layer • Reusable application framework services • Application Framework/s Technology Standardization
Enabling Technology Capabilities	Enterprise application framework/s need to have the following key IT enablers (but not limited to) thus enabling business capabilities to achieve strategic objectives: • Integration with web tier frameworks (e.g. Spring MVC, Struts, Tapestry) • Annotations based programming • Dependency Injections • Abstraction layer for transaction management • JDBC Abstraction layer • Integration with ORM Frameworks (e.g. Hibernate)

TABLE 5.54

(Continued)

Traceability	
Principles	The following set of Architecture Principles needs to be enforced from the Portal Framework selection through strategy to implementation: • **Prefer Use over Buy over Build** • **Drive for Reusable Solution Building Blocks** • **Avoid Current State Driving/Constraining Future State Design** • **Base Architecture on Service Orientation** • **Comply to Standards** • **Rationalize Technology** • **Delineate Architectural Responsibility**
Business Capability	The Enterprise application framework/s as part of foundation services are defined to contribute toward the following business capabilities. • Dynamic Content Management • Enterprise Solutions with Local Variants • Flexible Pricing and Quoting • Enterprise Customer Care • Enterprise Technology Planning and Cost-effective Operation (e.g. Application Framework Selection)
Architectural Observations	The following observation has identified the need for the Logging and Auditing Platform solution: • Technology Standardization • Emerging Technology Adoption

5.3.15 ORM Framework

Table 5.55 describes the ORM or data access Framework foundation service overview and its importance.

TABLE 5.55

Data Access Framework

Overview	ORM frameworks are standard set of libraries that has pre-built accelerators (e.g. Connection Factories, Query builder, Data Formatters, Paginated result) for data access services development. Enterprise ORM Framework/s is defined as part of foundation services in the Enterprise Architecture to address data access standards & guidelines and reusable data access/ORM framework catalog. Data Access/ORM framework can evolve as follows: • Define data access standards & guidelines and Data access/ORM framework catalog • Extend the ORM framework based on organization data access requirements and create reusable data services for the enterprise applications to reuse in their architecture
Need	ORM framework/s are needed to: • Avoid multiple custom data access solutions being built • Avoid inconsistent usage of multiple open source ORM framework/s • Enable Standardization of data services development • Adopt emerging technology in the data access layer • Improved separation of concerns between business service/application service and data services • Reusable data access services • Data Access Technology Standardization

(Continued)

TABLE 5.55

(Continued)

Enabling Technology Capabilities	Enterprise ORM Framework/s need to have the following key IT enablers (an dpotentially others) thus enabling business capabilities to achieve strategic objectives.

- Custom Query Language
- Annotations
- Mapping of Java Objects
- Audit functionality
- Standards—JPA 2.0, JDBC
- Declarative Data caching
- Cache Integration
- Application Framework integration (e.g. Spring)
- Code Generators
- Cross Platform (Java and.NET)
- Concurrent updates support through optimistic locking

Traceability

Principles	The following set of Architecture Principles needs to be enforced from the ORM Framework selection through strategy to implementation:

- **Prefer Use over Buy over Build**
- **Drive for Reusable Solution Building Blocks**
- **Avoid Current State Driving/Constraining Future State Design**
- **Base Architecture on Service Orientation**
- **Comply to Standards**
- **Rationalize Technology**
- **Secure Information**
- **Delineate Architectural Responsibility**

Business Capability	The Enterprise ORM Framework/s as part of foundation services are defined to contribute toward the following business capabilities.

- Dynamic Content Management
- Product Localization
- Flexible Pricing and Quoting
- Enterprise Content and Service Bundling
- Enterprise Customer Care
- 360 Degree Enterprise Customer View
- Enterprise Technology Planning and Cost-effective Operation (e.g. ORM Framework Selection)

Architectural Observations	The following observation has identified the need for the ORM Framework Platform solution.

- Data Services
- Technology Standardization
- Emerging Technology Adoption

5.3.16 Caching Framework

Table 5.56 describes the caching foundation service overview and its importance:

TABLE 5.56

Caching Foundation Service

Overview	Enterprise caching framework typically consists of a library that accelerates the data retrieval performance by caching the frequently accessed data in memory Enterprise caching framework/s is defined as part of foundation services in the Enterprise Architecture to provide common set of caching standards &guidelines and reusable cache implementation framework Based on the level of EA maturity adoption, Cache framework can evolve as described below: • Define caching standards & guidelines and Open Standard Cache framework catalog • Extend the open standard cache framework based on specific requirements of caching and create extended cache framework with reusable services for the applications to reuse in their architecture
Need	Enterprise Framework is needed to: • Avoid multiple custom cache solutions are being built within the organization • Enable standardization of cache Implementation • Adopt emerging technology in the cache implementation • Improved separation of concerns between application business logic and cache implementation • Reusable cache services • Cache technology standardization
Enabling Technology Capabilities	Enterprise Cache platform needs to have the following key IT enablers (but not limited to) thus enabling business capabilities to achieve strategic objectives. • Presentation layer cache • Business layer cache • Data access layer cache • Cache storage (in-memory and disk based) • Clustering Support • Caching of arbitrary objects • Pluggable refresh policies for expiry of cached item • API support for extending and customizing
Traceability	
Principles	The following set of Architecture Principles needs to be enforced from the Enterprise Cache Framework selection through strategy to implementation. • **Prefer Use over Buy over Build** • **Drive for Reusable Solution Building Blocks** • **Base Architecture on Service Orientation** • **Comply to Standards** • **Rationalize Technology** • **Secure Information**
Business Capability	The Enterprise Cache Framework as part of foundation services is defined to contribute toward the following business capabilities. • Dynamic Content Management • Product Localization • Flexible Pricing and Quoting • Enterprise Content and Service Bundling • Enterprise Customer Care • 360 Degree Enterprise Customer View • Enterprise Technology Planning and Cost-effective Operation (e.g. Cache Framework Selection)
Architectural Observations	The following observation has identified the need for the Logging and Auditing Platform solution. • Technology Standardization • Emerging Technology Adoption

5.3.17 Exception Management

Exception management is the Architecture Building Block envisaged to address centralized exception service as shown in Figure 5.18.

- Consumers include enterprise applications and services e.g. portal applications, process services, business services, batch services
- Concrete interfaces with multiple protocol support and binding
- Consists of key functions:
  - o To receive the exceptions, process and send it to appropriate workflow
  - o Notify the concerned people with right set of information
  - o Auto correction or manual correction
  - o Resubmit/Recovery to reinitiate the failure business process or service
  - o Role-based access user interface to work on the exceptions or view the exceptions
  - o Common canonicals for sending the log/audit events
  - o Libraries for distributed service

Table 5.57 describes the Exception Management Foundation Service overview and its importance:

5.3.18 Logging and Auditing

Logging and Auditing is the Architecture Building Block envisaged to address centralized logging and auditing service as shown in Figure 5.19.

- Consumers include enterprise applications and services e.g. portal applications, process services, business services, batch services

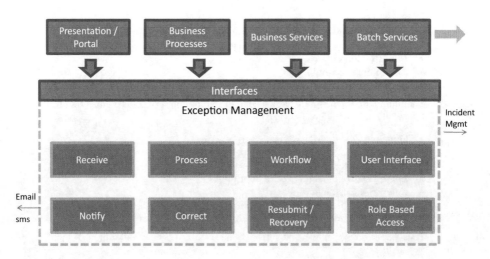

FIGURE 5.18
Exception Management—Conceptual View.

TABLE 5.57

Exception Management Foundation Service

Overview	Enterprise Exception Management is a standard framework solution that provides reusable library and centralized management console for resolving system/business-critical exceptions for operations to manage. Enterprise Exception Management framework is defined as part of foundation services in the Enterprise Architecture to address exception management standards & guidelines, standard exception XML schema, exception framework based on requirements. Based on the level of EA maturity adoption, Exception Management framework can be evolved as described below: • Define Exception management standards & guidelines, Canonical Exception Message XML and base Exception Framework library • Develop Centralized Exception management service which would receive business and system critical events to be notified to operations • Develop unified console for operations to acknowledge these critical events and route it to appropriate people using workflow
Need	Enterprise Exception Management Framework is needed to: • Avoid multiple Exception management solution are being used for the same functionality • Enable Standardization of Exception Management Framework • Improve separation of concerns between Application logic and handling of exception events • Eliminate time consuming manual interventions for ignorable exceptions • Reusable Exception Management Libraries • Better Operations Support

Enabling Technology Capabilities	Enterprise Exception Management Framework platform needs to have the following key IT enablers (and potentially others) thus enabling business capabilities to achieve strategic objectives:
	
	• Option to implement as standalone library as part of individual application or centralized reusable service
	• Centralized exception management for application exceptions and business exceptions
	• Integration with incident management system
	• Email alerts
	• Standard Exception XML Message
	• Web Services Support
	• Nice to have:
	  o Workflow functionality to route it appropriate persons
	  o SMS Alerts to appropriate people
	  o Auto correction

Traceability	
Principles	The following set of Architecture Principles needs to be enforced from the Enterprise Exception Management solution selection through strategy to implementation: • **Prefer Use over Buy over Build** • **Drive for Reusable Solution Building Blocks** • **Base Architecture on Service Orientation** • **Comply to Standards** • **Reduce Manual Interventions**
Business Capability	Not Applicable
Architectural Observations	The following observation has identified the need for the Exception Management solution: • Business process pain points due to application frequent issues • Technology Standardization • Emerging Technology Adoption

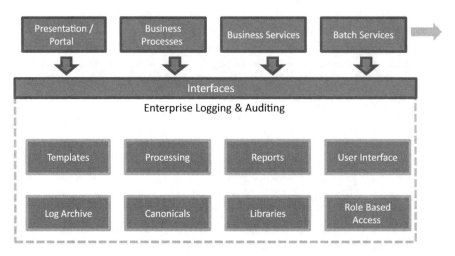

FIGURE 5.19
Enterprise Logging and Auditing—Conceptual View.

- Concrete interfaces with multiple protocol support and binding
- Consists of key functions:
  o Receive the logging and audit events, process and archive it
  o Role-based access user interface to view the log/audit reports
  o Reporting functionality
  o Templates for pattern recognition
  o Common canonicals for sending the log/audit events
  o Libraries for distributed service

Table 5.58 describes the Logging and Auditing foundation service overview and its importance.

TABLE 5.58

Logging and Auditing Foundation Service

Overview	Enterprise Logging and Auditing platform is a framework that provides common set of standards & guidelines, reusable implementation framework, Extendable Logging and Auditing canonical and runtime for centralized logging and auditing platform. Enterprise Logging and Auditing Platform are defined as part of foundation services in the Enterprise Architecture to address all requirements and concerns associated with application logging and auditing. Logging and Auditing can evolve as follows.
	• Define Standards & Guidelines that include criteria for logging and auditing, Logging and Auditing Standard XML schema (extendable), Open Standard framework
	• Extend the open standard framework and create reusable libraries for all the applications to reuse in their architecture
	• Provide Centralized Logging Service which could receive all the logging and auditing events asynchronously and process in a non-production environment.

TABLE 5.58

(Continued)

Need	Enterprise Logging Platform is needed to:

- Avoid multiple logging and auditing solutions being built
- Enable Logging and Auditing Standardization
- Adopt emerging technology in the logging and auditing
- Improved separation of concerns between application business logic and logging & auditing functionality
- Reusable Logging and Auditing services
- Centralized logging and auditing in a non-production environment

Enabling Technology Capabilities	Enterprise Logging and Auditing platform needs to have the following key IT enablers (but not limited to) thus enabling business capabilities to achieve strategic objectives.

- Open Standard framework for logging and auditing
- Centralized Logging and Auditing Infrastructure
- Event-based Logging and Auditing
- Supports multiple protocols to accept logging and auditing messages—Web SERVICES, JMS, MQ, FILE
- Archives the logged and audit messages into backup repository
- Support Non-blocking calls to improve the performance
- Standard canonical for log and audit message
- Support for extended Audit functionality
- Option to implement as standalone library as part of individual application or reusable service

Traceability	
Principles	The following set of Architecture Principles needs to be enforced from the Logging & Auditing Framework selection through strategy to implementation.

- **Prefer Use over Buy over Build**
- **Drive for Reusable Solution Building Blocks**
- **Avoid Current State Driving/Constraining Future State Design**
- **Base Architecture on Service Orientation**
- **Comply to Standards**
- **Rationalize Technology**
- **Secure Information**

Business Capability	The Enterprise Logging and Auditing Platform as part of foundation services is defined to contribute toward the following business capabilities.

- Enterprise Technology Planning and Cost-effective Operation (e.g. Logging and Auditing Framework Selection)

Architectural Observations	The following observation has identified the need for the Logging and Auditing Platform solution.

- Technology Standardization
- Emerging Technology Adoption

5.3.19 Notification Service

Notification Service is the Architecture Building Block envisaged to address centralized Notification Service as shown in Figure 5.20.

- Consumers include enterprise applications and services e.g. portal applications, process services, business services, batch services
- Concrete interfaces with multiple protocol support and binding

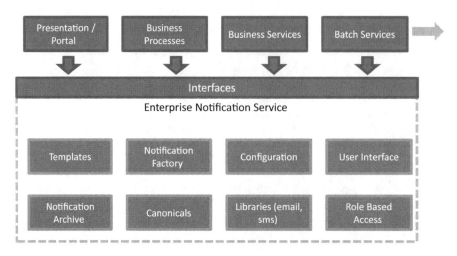

FIGURE 5.20
Notification Service—Conceptual View.

- Consists of key functions:
  - o Notification factory-based implementation for multiple channel notifications
  - o Receive the notification message and format it and send it to right destination
  - o Role-based access user interface to view the notification messages
  - o Configuration for notification parameters
  - o Templates for multiple format of notifications
  - o Common canonicals for sending the notification request and response
  - o Libraries for distributed service

Table 5.59 describes the Notification Foundation Service overview and its importance.

TABLE 5.59

Notification Foundation Service

Overview	Enterprise Notification Service is a solution that provides common set of standards & guidelines, reusable implementation framework, Extendable Notification canonical and runtime for centralized event-based notification service platform. Enterprise Notification Service is defined as part of foundation services in the Enterprise Architecture to address the requirements and concerns associated with application notification requirements and alerts. Based on the level of maturity adoption, Notification Service can evolve as follows: • Define Standards & Guidelines that include guidelines for Notification Channels, Notification Standard XML schema (extendable) • Develop Notification base framework with extendable option and create reusable libraries for all the applications to reuse in their architecture • Provide Centralized Event-based Notification Service which could receive notification events asynchronously and process separately.

TABLE 5.59

(Continued)

Need	Enterprise Notification Framework and Service is needed to:

- Avoid multiple Notification Framework solutions are being built
- Enable Notification Method Standardization
- Adopt emerging technology in the Notification Framework development
- Improved separation of concerns between application business logic and notification functionality
- Reusable Notification Framework and services (e.g. SendEmail, SendSMS)
- Centralized Notification Service Platform

Enabling Technology Capabilities	Enterprise Notification platform needs to have the following key IT enablers (but not limited to) thus enabling business capabilities to achieve strategic objectives.

- Option to implement as standalone library as part of individual application or reusable service
- Built using Open Standard technologies such as Java, JMS and Web Services
- Adapt Abstract factory design pattern to support multiple notification service implementation
- Standard xml schema for notification message with extendable option
- Standard Service interfaces to provide separation of concerns
- Event-based Notification Events
- Supports multiple protocols to accept notification messages—Web Service, JMS, MQ and FILE
- Archives the notification event messages into backup repository
- Support Non-blocking calls to improve the performance

Traceability

Principles	The following set of Architecture Principles needs to be enforced from the Notification Framework selection through strategy to implementation:

- **Prefer Use over Buy over Build**
- **Drive for Reusable Solution Building Blocks**
- **Avoid Current State Driving/Constraining Future State Design**
- **Base Architecture on Service Orientation**
- **Comply to Standards**
- **Rationalize Technology**
- **Secure Information**

Business Capability	The Enterprise Notification Service as part of foundation services is defined to contribute toward the following business capabilities.

- All the business capabilities that has impact with business processes and business services which uses notification functionality
- Enterprise Technology Planning and Cost-effective Operation (e.g. Notification Service Selection)

Architectural Observations	The following observation has identified the need for the Logging and Auditing Platform solution:

- Pain points due to inflexible configurations
- Technology Standardization
- Emerging Technology Adoption

5.3.20 BRMS

Business Rules Management is the Architecture Building Block envisaged to address rules management service as shown in Figure 5.21.

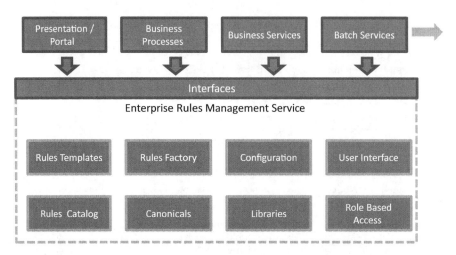

FIGURE 5.21
Business Rules Management—Conceptual View.

- Consumers include enterprise applications and services e.g. portal applications, process services, business services, batch services
- Concrete interfaces with multiple protocol support and binding
- Consists of key functions:
    o Rules factory-based implementation for multiple types of rules
    o Receive the rules execution request and execute to provide the response to caller
    o Role-based access with business user interface to manage the rules
    o Configuration for rules parameters
    o Templates for multiple types of rules to accelerate development
    o Rules catalog for persisting the rules
    o Common canonicals for rules request and response
    o Libraries for distributed service

Table 5.60 describes the Rules management service overview and its importance.

5.3.21 Scheduler

Table 5.61 describes the Scheduler foundation service overview and its importance.

5.3.22 Document Management

Table 5.62 describes the Document Management foundation service overview and its importance.

TABLE 5.60

Business Rules Management Service

Overview	Business Rules Management is a solution that provides common platform for managing business rules with configurable parameters to integrate with application business logic for seamless execution of compiled business rules. BRMS Platform is defined as part of foundation services in the Enterprise Architecture to address common set of business rules development standards & guidelines, reusable implementation BRMS framework, runtime for Business rules execution platform and business rules development platform. BRMS can evolve as described below: • Define Standards & Guidelines that include criteria for buses development and usage, Business Rules Standard Templates, Open Standard Business Rules framework • Extend the open standard framework and create reusable services and libraries for all the applications to reuse and extend based on their need in their architecture • Provide Centralized Business Rules Management Platform which could expose each application business rules as a service or API package and provide standard interface specifications for creating business rules.
Need	BRMS Platform is needed to: • Avoid business rules being hard-coded or rigid programming language • Avoid multiple business rules solutions being built in the enterprise • Enable standardization of business rules development and management • Adopt emerging technology in the business rules platform • Improved separation of concerns for the business logics which are potential candidate for dynamic change due to market demand • Reusable business rules services (e.g. approval thresholds)

Enabling Technology Capabilities	BRMS platform needs to have the following key IT enablers (but not limited to) thus enabling business capabilities to achieve strategic objectives.
	• Rule execution engine—execution, sequencing and chaining of rules, and event-based execution
	• Rule repository
	• Model rules, simulation, identify the dependencies between rules and performance tracking
	• Dynamic addition/deletion of rules
	• Rule management and administration—promotion between development, test and production environments, and track changes and performance
	• Integrated development environment
	• Business user friendly interface
	• Integration
	  • BPM Tool and ESB Integration
	  • Integrates with multiple databases, XML documents, Java objects,.NET/COM objects, and COBOL copybooks
	• Performance—Fast response time in executing the rule (e.g. supports Rete III inference engine)
	• SOA—Web Services, event-based and rule can be exposed as services

(Continued)

TABLE 5.60
(Continued)

Traceability Principles	The following set of Architecture Principles needs to be enforced from the BRMS solution selection through strategy to implementation: • **Prefer Use over Buy over Build** • **Set Up Enterprise Solutions with Local Variants** • **Drive for Reusable Solution Building Blocks** • **Base Architecture on Service Orientation** • **Comply to Standards** • **Rationalize Technology** • **Reduce Manual Interventions**
Business Capability	The BRMS as part of foundation services is defined to contribute toward the following business capabilities. • Flexible pricing and quoting (e.g. configurable price models through business rules) • Dynamic content management • Product localization • Enterprise content and service bundling • Enterprise technology planning and cost-effective operation (e.g. BRMS Platform Selection)
Architectural Observations	The following observation has identified the need for the BRMS Platform solution: • Application functionality to frequently changed business logic and configuration that can be externalized • Technology standardization • Emerging technology adoption

TABLE 5.61

Scheduler Foundation Service

Overview	Enterprisescheduling solution is a standard library that provides time driven or event driven schedules for invoking any executable to perform business task in the back ground (e.g. batch processing of EDI orders). Enterprise Scheduling framework is defined as part of foundation services in the Enterprise Architecture to provide scheduling standards & guidelines, open standard scheduler solution and extended framework. Based on the level of EA maturity adoption, Scheduling framework can be evolved as described below: • Define scheduling standards & guidelines and scheduler solution • Extend the Scheduler solution based on specific job scheduling requirements to create framework, enhance standards and guidelines and develop potential reusable scheduling services for the applications to reuse in their architecture
Need	Enterprise Scheduler Framework is needed to: • Avoid multiple job schedulers are being used for the same technology • Avoid multiple custom scheduling solutions are being built • Enable Standardization of Scheduling framework • Adopt emerging technology in the Scheduling solution • Improved separation of concerns between job invocation and Job Execution • Reusable Scheduler services (e.g. Delete Schedule, Create Schedule, Run Schedule, get JobRunHistory) • Scheduler technology standardization
Enabling Technology Capabilities	Enterprise Scheduler platform needs to have the following key IT enablers (and potentially others) thus enabling business capabilities to achieve strategic objectives. • Application container support (JEE or.NET) • Run as a Standalone program within JVM or.NET container • Can be embedded in another standalone application (Java or.NET) • Can run on Clusters with failover capabilities • Multiple types of triggers to execute Job (e.g. time of day—up to minutes, days of week/month/year, business day calendar support, recurrence) • Job groups, Trigger groups • Job Execution through interface • Success/failure through response code • Support for sending response to Listener interfaces • Configurable actions based on Job completion code • Plug-in support to extend the scheduler functionality • Monitoring and administration Console • Participate in two phase commit transaction • Support for database persistence of job executions

(Continued)

TABLE 5.61

(Continued)

Traceability	
Principles	The following set of Architecture Principles needs to be enforced from the Enterprise Scheduler platform selection through strategy to implementation: • **Prefer Use over Buy over Build** • **Drive for Reusable Solution Building Blocks** • **Base Architecture on Service Orientation** • **Comply to Standards** • **Rationalize Technology** • **Reduce Manual Interventions**
Business Capability	The Enterprise Scheduling Framework as part of foundation services is defined to contribute toward the following business capabilities. • All other business capabilities which has impact to business processes that uses time driven or event driven executable business functions through job scheduling • Enterprise Technology Planning and Cost-effective Operation (e.g. Scheduler Solution Selection)
Architectural Observations	The following observation has identified the need for the Scheduler solution: • Automation of Job executions (e.g. most of the jobs are script driven and not automated) • Technology Standardization • Emerging Technology Adoption

TABLE 5.62

Document Management Foundation Service

Overview	Document management solution is a set of services that provides store, retrieval, search, metadata management associated with documents. It also overlaps with functionality of content management domain. Document management framework is defined as part of foundation services in the Enterprise Architecture to provide standards & guidelines, open standard document management solution and extended framework based on y requirements. Based on the level of EA maturity adoption, document management framework can be evolved as described below: • Define document management standards & guidelines and framework for document management
Need	Enterprise Document Management Framework is needed to: • Avoid multiple document management solutions are being used for the same technology • Avoid multiple custom document management solutions are being built • Enable Standardization of Document management framework • Adopt emerging technology in the Document management solution • Improved separation of concerns between application business logic and document handling functionality • Reusable Document management services (e.g. CRUD Services of Document, Search Document, Manage Metadata) • Document Management Technology standardization
Enabling Technology Capabilities	Enterprise Document Management platform needs to have the following key IT enablers (but not limited to) thus enabling business capabilities to achieve strategic objectives. • Application container support (JEE or.NET) • Run as a Standalone program within JVM or.NET container • Can be embedded in another standalone application (Java or.NET) • Can run on Clusters with failover capabilities • Capture through OCR, Store in File systems or database, hierarchy support • Indexing with metadata and Search capability • Distribution and Retrieval • Workflow and Security • Versioning
Traceability	
Principles	The following set of Architecture Principles needs to be enforced from the Enterprise Document Management platform selection through strategy to implementation: • **Prefer Use over Buy over Build** • **Drive for Reusable Solution Building Blocks** • **Base Architecture on Service Orientation** • **Comply to Standards** • **Rationalize Technology** • **Reduce Manual Interventions**
Business Capability	The Enterprise Document Management Framework as part of foundation services is defined to contribute toward the following business capabilities. • All other business capabilities which has impact to business processes that uses document management functions • Enterprise Technology Planning and Cost-effective Operation (e.g. Document management solution Selection)
Architectural Observations	The following observation has identified the need for the Scheduler solution: • Avoid manual interventions in document handling • Technology Standardization • Emerging Technology Adoption

5.3.23 Workflow Management

Table 5.63 describes the Workflow foundation service overview and its importance.

TABLE 5.63

Workflow Foundation Service

Overview	Enterprise Workflow Management solution is a standard service that provides functionality for creating people workflow (approve, delegate, re-route and reject) to perform different types of business tasks in seamless manner. Workflow management is defined as part of foundation services in the Enterprise Architecture to provide workflow standards & guidelines, open standard workflow solution and extended framework based on requirements. Based on the level of EA maturity adoption, Workflow Management framework can be evolved as described below.
	• Define Workflow standards & guidelines and Workflow Management solution (BPM solution has overlap with workflow functionality) • Extend the Workflow Management solution based on specific workflow requirements and BPM product selection to create framework, enhance standards and guidelines and develop potential reusable workflow services for the applications to reuse in their architecture
Need	Enterprise Workflow management is needed to:
	• Avoid multiple Workflow Frameworks are being used for the same technology • Avoid multiple custom Workflow solutions are being built • Enable Standardization of Workflow management framework • Adopt emerging technology in the Workflow solution • Improved separation of concerns between Application business logic and workflow framework • Reusable Workflow management services (e.g. Create Workflow, Approve Workflow, Reject, Delegate) • Workflow Management Technology standardization
Enabling Technology Capabilities	Enterprise Workflow Management needs to have the following key IT enablers (but not limited to) thus enabling business capabilities to achieve strategic objectives.
	• Application container support (JEE or.NET) • Run as a Standalone program within JVM or.NET container • Can be embedded in another standalone application (Java or.NET) • Can run on Clusters with failover capabilities • Standards support (e.g. BPMN, BPEL, JPDL) • Task Management
Traceability	
Principles	The following set of Architecture Principles needs to be enforced from the Enterprise Workflow platform selection through strategy to implementation:
	• **Prefer Use over Buy over Build** • **Drive for Reusable Solution Building Blocks** • **Base Architecture on Service Orientation** • **Comply to Standards** • **Rationalize Technology** • **Reduce Manual Interventions**

(Continued)

TABLE 5.63

(Continued)

Business Capability	The Enterprise Scheduling Framework as part of foundation services is defined to contribute toward the following business capabilities.
	• All other business capabilities which has impact to business processes that uses Workflow functionality • Enterprise Technology Planning and Cost-effective Operation (e.g. Scheduler Solution Selection)
Architectural Observations	The following observation has identified the need for the Workflow Management solution:
	• Recurrent process steps are driven manually (candidate for workflow automation) • Technology Standardization • Emerging Technology Adoption

5.3.24 Security

Security is the Architecture Building Block responsible for supporting SSO, Authentication, Authorization and Digital security functionalities that are required to fulfill the security requirements in the enterprise architecture.

Table 5.64 details the security platform and its importance from enterprise architecture perspective.

TABLE 5.64

Security Platform

Overview	Security solution is a shared service that would serve as a one-stop for all security related requirements to be addressed in user interaction or application interaction. Security is considered as shared service platform to provide identity management, access management, SSO and digital security functionalities. Security is defined as part of share services layer in the Enterprise Architecture since it provides the functionality that cross cuts all the layers and building blocks within layers. Securing web services is a special perspective that becomes relevant in a service world
Need	Security as shared service platform is needed to:
	• Avoid multiple security solution being built for the similar functionality • Centralized management of identity, access, SSO and other security related functionalities could be cost-effective • Adopting to emerging technology in the security space • Improved separation of concerns between application and security requirements • Reusable security services (e.g. SSO plug-in, authentication framework, entitlement or authorization management, digital security—signing, certificate validation, de-signing)
Enabling Technology Capabilities	Enterprise security platform needs to have the following key IT enablers (but not limited to) thus enabling business capabilities to achieve strategic objectives.
	• Integration with identity Storage • SSO Support • Authentication and Authorization • Digital Security Support • Centralized application security and authorization • Support for JEE App integration

(Continued)

TABLE 5.64

(Continued)

	• Self-Service password management • Standards support (SAML, WS-Federation, OAUTH etc.) • Cluster, Load balance, Dynamic Failover • Auditing and Logging • OOTB support for Web Services typically through Policies
Traceability	
Principles	The following set of Architecture Principles needs to be enforced from the security platform selection through strategy to implementation: • **Prefer Use over Buy over Build** • **Drive for Reusable Solution Building Blocks** • **Avoid Current State Driving/Constraining Future State Design** • **Delineate Architectural Responsibility** • **Base Architecture on Service Orientation** • **Comply to Standards** • **Rationalize Technology** • **Secure Information**
Business Capability	The Enterprise Security Platform as part of Shared Service Layer is defined to contribute toward the following business capabilities. • Enterprise Customer Care (e.g. role-based access for Customer Care, Seamless login into multiple applications) • 360 Degree Enterprise Customer View (e.g. Entitlements on Data from multiple data sources) • Enterprise approach to partner piloting, implementation and integration (e.g. Partner User Access, Vendor application integration) • Enterprise Technology Planning and Cost-effective Operation (e.g. Security platform Selection)
Architectural Observations	The following observation has identified the need for Security Platform solution. • Global Identity Management • Federated Access Management • Authentication and Authorization

5.3.25 Mobile Services

Mobile Services refers to the Architecture Building Blocks responsible for supporting enterprise application development and runtime platform for mobile platform requirements in the enterprise architecture.

Table 5.65 details the Mobile Services platform overview and its importance.

5.3.26 IVR Services

IVR Services are architecture building block/s responsible for enabling IVR development and runtime platform that are required to fulfill IVR channel requirements in the enterprise architecture.

Table 5.66 details the IVR Services platform overview and its importance.

TABLE 5.65

Mobile Services Platform

Overview	Enterprise Mobile Services Platform is a framework service that provides standards, frameworks/reusable libraries, development and run time platform for Mobile channel development (Mobile Web Client, iPhone apps, Android Apps, Tablets etc.). Enterprise Mobiles Service is defined as part of framework services layer in the Enterprise Architecture since it provides the Mobile Development standards and guidelines, Mobile Reusable Services, Runtime Platform that cross cuts all the building blocks within portal layer.
Need	Enterprise Mobile Services as Framework service platform is needed to: <ul><li>Avoid multiple Mobile solutions are being used</li><li>Enable Standardization of Mobile Services development and Deployment</li><li>Centralized Mobile Services management</li><li>Adopting to emerging technology in the Mobile Services solution</li><li>Improved separation of concerns between application and Mobile channel requirements</li><li>Potential Reusable Common Mobile services</li><li>Enabling niche features of Mobile Platform to support futuristic requirements</li></ul>
Enabling Technology Capabilities	Enterprise Mobile platform needs to have the following key IT enablers (but not limited to) thus enabling business capabilities to achieve strategic objectives. <ul><li>IDE for Mobile native application development—includes code debugging, WYSIWYG Editors, Form builders, desktop-based</li><li>Application Management and Security</li><li>Enterprise Application Integration—database, API, XML and SQL tools, pre-build libraries</li><li>Device and OS Support</li><li>Cross platform support (Apple, Andriod, RIM, Symbhion, Windows)</li><li>Offline access with cached support</li><li>Thin client and thick client support</li></ul>
Traceability	
Principles	The following set of Architecture Principles needs to be enforced from the Mobile Service platform selection through strategy to implementation: <ul><li>**Prefer Use over Buy over Build**</li><li>**Drive for Reusable Solution Building Blocks**</li><li>**Delineate Architectural Responsibility**</li><li>**Base Architecture on Service Orientation**</li><li>**Comply to Standards**</li><li>**Rationalize Technology**</li><li>**Secure Information**</li></ul>
Business Capability	The Enterprise Mobile Services Platform as part of Shared Service Layer is defined to contribute toward the following business capabilities. <ul><li>Enterprise Customer Care</li><li>360 Degree Enterprise Customer View</li><li>Enterprise Technology Planning and Cost-effective Operation (e.g. Mobile Services platform Selection)</li></ul>
Architectural Observations	The following observation has identified the need for Mobile Services Platform solution: <ul><li>Pain points due to absence of Customer Access through mobile and other devices</li><li>Technology Rationalization</li></ul>

TABLE 5.66

IVR Services Platform

Overview	Enterprise IVR Services Platform is a framework and shared service that provides development and run time platform for customer interactions through IVR channel. Enterprise IVR Service is defined as part of shared services layer in the Enterprise Architecture since it provides the standards and guidelines, IVR Reusable Services, Runtime Platform that cross cuts all the building blocks within portal layer.
Need	Enterprise IVR Solution as shared service platform is needed to: • Avoid multiple IVR solutions are being used • Enable Standardization of IVR development and Deployment • Centralized IVR Services management • Adopting to emerging technology in the IVR solution • Improved separation of concerns between application and IVR channel requirements • Potential Reusable Common IVR services
Enabling Technology Capabilities	Enterprise IVR platform needs to have the following key IT enablers (but not limited to) thus enabling business capabilities to achieve strategic objectives. • Real-time and historical reports and integration with third part reporting products • Web based administration interface • Geographical Redundancy with high availability • Development of IVR Flows through desktop-based solution • RDBMS support • Integration with Network Management solution • Integration with LDAP
Traceability	
Principles	The following set of Architecture Principles needs to be enforced from the IVR platform selection through strategy to implementation: • **Prefer Use over Buy over Build** • **Drive for Reusable Solution Building Blocks** • **Delineate Architectural Responsibility** • **Base Architecture on Service Orientation** • **Comply to Standards** • **Rationalize Technology** • **Secure Information**
Business Capability	The Enterprise IVR Platform as part of Shared Service Layer is defined to contribute toward the following business capabilities. • Enterprise Customer Care • 360 Degree Enterprise Customer View • Enterprise Technology Planning and Cost-effective Operation (e.g. IVR platform Selection).
Architectural Observations	The following observation has identified the need for IVR Platform solution. • Pain points due to absence of self-service functionality • Rationalize Technology

5.3.27 Reporting

Reporting is the Architecture Building Block responsible for managing development and runtime reporting platform required to fulfill the reporting requirements in the enterprise architecture.

Table 5.67 details the Reporting platform overview and its importance.

TABLE 5.67

Reporting Platform

Overview	Enterprise Reporting Platform is a shared service that provides reporting development platform, standards and guidelines, Reporting runtime platform for other enterprise applications. Enterprise Reporting is defined as part of shared services layer in the Enterprise Architecture since it provides the functionality that cross cuts all the building blocks within process and business service layer.
Need	Enterprise Reporting Solution as shared service platform is needed to: • Avoid multiple reporting solutions are being built • Enable Standardization of Report development and Deployment • Centralized report management that include access, data sources, template layout and delivery • Adopting to emerging technology in the Reporting solution • Improved separation of concerns between application and reporting requirements • Enable niche features (custom reporting, pre-built templates, multi-format delivery etc.) • Reusable Common Reporting services (e.g. Order Reports, Customer Data Report, Product related reports)
Enabling Technology Capabilities	Enterprise Reporting platform needs to have the following key IT enablers (but not limited to) thus enabling business capabilities to achieve strategic objectives. • Pre-built templates for faster development of reports • Integration support for disparate data sources on heterogeneous platforms • Rich Presentation through readymade widgets, tables, graphs, charts • Rich Data Format and Layout format support • Integration with Business Intelligence platform • Administration Console • Role-based administration console • Role-based Data security • Authentication using SSO • Clustering and Scalability support
Traceability	
Principles	The following set of Architecture Principles needs to be enforced from the Enterprise Report platform selection through strategy to implementation: • **Prefer Use over Buy over Build** • **Drive for Reusable Solution Building Blocks** • **Avoid Current State Driving/Constraining Future State Design** • **Delineate Architectural Responsibility** • **Base Architecture on Service Orientation** • **Comply to Standards** • **Rationalize Technology** • **Secure Information**
Business Capability	The Enterprise Reporting Platform as part of Shared Service Layer is defined to contribute toward the following business capabilities. • Dynamic Content Management (e.g. Content QA Report) • Product Localization (e.g. Multi-language reports) • Enterprise Customer Care (e.g. Customer Details Report) • 360 Degree Enterprise Customer View (e.g. Customer Profile Report) • Time-to-Market and Performance Measurement (e.g. Product Performance Report) • Enterprise Strategic Sourcing and Vendor Management • Enterprise Partnership Management • Enterprise Technology Planning and Cost-effective Operation (e.g. Reporting platform Selection)
Current State Observations	The following observation has identified the need for Reporting Platform solution. • Technology Rationalization • Custom Reports and Pre-built templates

5.3.28 Business Analytics

Business Analytics refers to the Architecture Building Block responsible for providing development and runtime analytical platform that are required to fulfill the analytical requirements in the enterprise architecture.

Table 5.68 details the business analytics platform overview and its importance.

TABLE 5.68

Business Analytics Platform

Overview	Enterprise business analytics is part of BI Platform which is a shared service that provides development and runtime platform business analytics (not specific to any functionality) for all the LOBs which need analytics functionality. Enterprise business analytics is defined as part of share services layer in the Enterprise Architecture since it provides the analytics functionality that cross cuts all the building blocks within business and process orchestration layer
Need	Business Analytics is defined as part of BI as shared service platform is needed to:
	• Avoid multiple Business analytics solution being built for the same functionality • Adopting to emerging technology in the Business analytics • Improved separation of concerns between application and analytical requirements • Reusable business analytics services (e.g. Product Performance, Sale Performance for particular type of customer)
Enabling Technology Capabilities	Enterprise business analytics platform needs to have the following key IT enablers (but not limited to) thus enabling business capabilities to achieve strategic objectives.
	• Social and content analytics • Integration—business rules, ESB, web services, social software, MDM • Development tools—SDK and wizard support • Support for extreme data performance—in-memory processing • On-demand scalability • Decision platform • BI embedded in business process • Emerging data sources support such as Hadoop, Hive and NoSQL
Traceability	
Principles	The following set of Architecture Principles needs to be enforced from the business analytics platform selection through strategy to implementation.
	• **Prefer Use over Buy over Build** • **Drive for Reusable Solution Building Blocks** • **Avoid Current State Driving/Constraining Future State Design** • **Delineate Architectural Responsibility** • **Base Architecture on Service Orientation** • **Comply to Standards** • **Rationalize Technology** • **Secure Information** • **Maintain Gold Copy of Data**

TABLE 5.68

(Continued)

Business Capability	The Enterprise business analytics Platform as part of Shared Service Layer is defined to contribute toward the following business capabilities.
	• 360 Degree Enterprise Customer View • Time-to-Market and Performance Measurement • Enterprise Strategic Sourcing and Vendor Management • Enterprise Partnership Management • Enterprise Technology Planning and Cost-effective Operation (e.g. Business Analytics platform Selection)
Architectural Observations	The following observation has identified the need for business analytics Platform solution.
	• Enterprise Business Intelligence platform • Technology Rationalization

5.3.29 Business Activity Monitoring

Table 5.69 details the Business Activity Monitoring (BAM) platform overview and its importance.

TABLE 5.69

Business Activity Monitoring (BAM) Platform

Overview	BAM is a solution that supports business analytics shared service to provide analytical events collected from any data sources which include business processes, business services, integration services and data services. BAM is defined as part of BI in the shared services layer in the Enterprise Architecture since it provides the functionality that cross cuts Process, Business Service, Data layers and building blocks within those layers.
Need	Enterprise BAM as part of BI platform is needed to:
	• Avoid multiple BAM solutions are being built for the same functionality • Pro-actively monitor the business process performance in terms of business value • Adopt emerging technologies in BAM area (real-time events, multi-protocol support, rich dash boards etc.) • Standard BAM development platform
Enabling Technology Capabilities	Enterprise BAM platform needs to have the following key IT enablers (but not limited to) thus enabling business capabilities to achieve strategic objectives:
	• Multi-protocol and multi-format support for collecting data from heterogeneous data sources • Integration of ESB • Standard development platform for creating event collection, correlation, reporting • Support for integrating rules engine to perform event processing • Proactive monitoring through pattern detection • Support for multiple data types during processing of events • Integration with reporting engine and BI platform • Data Visualization through rich dashboards (widgets, graphs, charts etc.) • Support for actionable events • Informational and actionable alerts through email, web, SMS etc. • Role-based administration console • Role-based data security • Authentication using SSO • Clustering and Scalability support

(Continued)

TABLE 5.69

(Continued)

Traceability	
Principles	The following set of Architecture Principles needs to be enforced from the BAM platform selection through strategy to implementation. • **Prefer Use over Buy over Build** • **Drive for Reusable Solution Building Blocks** • **Avoid Current State Driving/Constraining Future State Design** • **Delineate Architectural Responsibility** • **Base Architecture on Service Orientation** • **Comply to Standards** • **Rationalize Technology** • **Secure Information**
Business Capability	The Enterprise BAM Platform as part of Shared Service Layer is defined to contribute toward the following business capabilities. • Enterprise customer care (e.g. customer issues monitoring) • 360 degree enterprise customer view (e.g. All types of customer tracking through BAM) • Enterprise Technology Planning and Cost-effective Operation (e.g. BAM platform Selection)
Architectural Observations	The following observation has identified the need for BAM Platform solution. • Technology rationalization • Emerging technology adoption

5.3.30 Web Analytics

Table 5.70 details the Web Analytics platform overview and its importance.

TABLE 5.70

Web Analytics Platform

Overview	Web Analytics solution is part of BI Platform which is considered as a shared service that provides development and runtime platform for Web Analytics (not specific to any functionality) for all the LOBs which need Web Analytics functionality Web Analytics is defined as part of shared services layer in the Enterprise Architecture since it provides the functionality that cross cuts most of the portals within presentation layer.
Need	Web Analytics as shared service platform is needed to: • Avoid multiple Web Analytics solutions being built for the same functionality • Enable standardization of Web Analytics platform • Adopting to emerging technology in Web Analytics area(Mobile, Tablet, RIA application tracking etc.) • Improve separation of concerns between application and Web Analytics solution • Enabling niche features such as Analytics intelligence, real-time reporting • Improve performance for large volume of records • Reusable Analytic services (e.g. Customer Product Usage, Activity Tracking, Customer Trend)

TABLE 5.70

(Continued)

Enabling Technology Capabilities	Enterprise Web Analytics platform needs to have the following key IT enablers (but not limited to) thus enabling business capabilities to achieve strategic objectives.
	
	• Data
	   • Multiple data sources integration through real-time or Batch feed
	   • Supportive tools for data quality and accuracy
	   • Data export
	   • Rich Media Tracking (e.g. Flash, Video, Social Networking, Silverlight tracking)
	   • Mobile Application Tracking (e.g. Track mobile websites, mobile apps and web-enabled mobile devices)
	   • Complete campaign tracking capabilities (e.g. Track email campaigns)
	   • Shopping Cart Tracking (e.g. Trace transactions)
	   • Advanced Segmentation
	   • Custom Variables
	   • Bench Marking
	• Reporting and Analysis
	   • Real-time reporting
	   • Advanced Analysis Tools
	   • Data Visualization, Custom Reports and Dashboards
	   • Analytics Intelligence
	   • Predictive analytics
	   • Data import/export through Web services or APIs
	   • Data Analysis (Scenario/funnel, OLAP)
	• API and developer platform
	   • Email Integration and Administration interfaces

Traceability	
Principles	The following set of Architecture Principles needs to be enforced for identification of the Web Analytics solution. These Principles need to be adhered to through strategy to implementation. • **Prefer Use over Buy over Build** • **Drive for Reusable Solution Building Blocks** • **Avoid Current State Driving/Constraining Future State Design** • **Delineate Architectural Responsibility** • **Base Architecture on Service Orientation** • **Comply to Standards** • **Rationalize Technology** • **Secure Information**
Business Capability	The Enterprise Web Analytics as part BI Shared Service Layer is defined to contribute toward the following business capabilities. • 360 Degree Enterprise Customer View (e.g. Customer Product usage Tracking) • Enterprise Technology Planning and Cost-effective Operation (e.g. Web Analytics platform Selection)
Architectural Observations	The following observation has identified the impact for Global Web Analytics Platform solution. • Technology Rationalization • Handling of large volume of data • Custom Reporting

5.3.31 Enterprise Search

Enterprise Search is the Architecture Building Block responsible for providing development and runtime analytical platform that are required to fulfill the analytical requirements in the enterprise architecture.

Table 5.71 details the Enterprise Search platform and its importance.

TABLE 5.71

Enterprise Search Platform

Overview	Enterprise Search is a shared service that would serve as one-stop for all searches related requirements in portal or business service layer.
	Enterprise Search is considered as shared service platform to provide content related search, document search, people search and transaction data, customer data, product data search and more.
	Enterprise Search is defined as part of share services layer in the Enterprise Architecture since it provides the functionality that cross cuts all the building blocks in the portal and business Service layers.
Need	Enterprise search as shared service platform is needed to:
	• Avoid multiple Enterprise Search COTS or Custom solution are being built for the similar functionality
	• Enable Standardization of Search Services development
	• Adopting to emerging technology for enterprise search solution
	• Improved separation of concerns between application and search requirements
	• Reusable Enterprise Search services (e.g. Content Search, product search, customer search, Employee Search, Document Search)
Enabling Technology Capabilities	Enterprise Search platform needs to have the following key IT enablers (and potentially others) thus enabling business capabilities to achieve strategic objectives:
	• Crawling
	• Thira party web sites, password protected contents, duplicate removal
	• Indexing multiple file types that includes HTML, PDF and MS Office documents
	• Multi-Language support
	• Filtering through file types, meta tags, websites etc.
	• Form based authentication
	• Proxy Server Support
	• Open Standards support
	• Sorting—relevance ranking, sort by date, sort by alphabetical order, sort order
	• Results—Highlighting PDF hits, dynamic summary, Query terms highlighted
	• Integration—Indexing API, XML Search Results output through API call
	• Search Queries
	• Spelling suggestions, Enable/Disable Stemming
	• Concept Search, wildcards support
	• Administration
	• Web based admin console and Reporting
	• Remote Management
	• Full replication and mirroring
	• Web based Reports
Traceability	
Principles	The following set of Architecture Principles need to be enforced while the Enterprise Search platform is selected and continuously to be adhered with these principles from enterprise search strategy to implementation:

TABLE 5.71

(Continued)

	• **Prefer Use over Buy over Build** • **Drive for Reusable Solution Building Blocks** • **Avoid Current State Driving/Constraining Future State Design** • **Delineate Architectural Responsibility** • **Base Architecture on Service Orientation** • **Comply to Standards** • **Rationalize Technology** • **Secure Information** • **Set Up Enterprise Solutions with Local Variants** (e.g. Location aware search results)
Business Capability	The Enterprise Search Platform as part of Shared Service Layer is defined to contribute toward the following business capabilities. • Enterprise Customer Care (e.g. role-based access for Customer Care, Seamless login into multiple applications) • 360 Degree enterprise customer view (e.g. Entitlements on data from multiple data sources) • Enterprise approach to partner piloting, implementation and integration (e.g. Partner User Access, Vendor application integration) • Enterprise Technology Planning and Cost-effective Operation (e.g. Security platform Selection)
Architectural Observations	The following observation has identified the need for Enterprise Search Platform solution. • Technology Rationalization and Standardization • Emerging Technology Adoption

5.3.32 Managed File Transfer

Managed File Transfer is the Architecture Building Block in the integration arena responsible for enabling automated file transfer management in the enterprise architecture.

Table 5.72 details the Managed File Transfer platform from shared service perspective.

TABLE 5.72

Managed File Transfer

Overview	MFT solution is a shared service that addresses the automated file transfer for any data transfer through file. MFT is defined as part of share services layer in the Enterprise Architecture since it provides the centralized management of file transfer, Service-based file transfer that cross cuts integration and business and data access layers and building blocks within layers. MFT works closely with integration platform.
Need	MFT as shared service platform is needed to: • Avoid script-based file transfers or native file transfer that leads to transfer failure which needs manual intervention • Enable centralized management of file transfer to save maintenance cost • Adopting to emerging technology in the File transfer management • Reusable File Transfer services (e.g. Order Management Sending Sale Details in Batch file through automated transfer)

(Continued)

TABLE 5.72

(Continued)

Enabling Technology Capabilities	Enterprise MFT platform needs to include the following key IT enablers (among others) thus enabling business capabilities to achieve strategic objectives. • Centralized management capability for all file transfers • Open standards adoption • Schedule, adhoc, event-based • Reliability—guaranteed delivery of files between applications • Service interface definition and messaging models for file transfers • Communication (routing, HTTP,HTTPS,FTP,FTPS, SFTP and proprietary) • Recovery—checkpoint restart • Integration—ESB, protocol transformation, data translation, JEE support • Security—authentication
Traceability	
Principles	The following set of Architecture Principles needs to be enforced from the platform selection through strategy to implementation: • **Prefer Use over Buy over Build** • **Drive for Reusable Solution Building Blocks** • **Avoid Current State Driving/Constraining Future State Design** • **Delineate Architectural Responsibility** • **Base Architecture on Service Orientation** • **Comply to Standards** • **Rationalize Technology** • **Secure Information** • **Reduce Manual Interventions**
Business Capability	The Enterprise MFT Platform as part of Shared Service Layer is defined to contribute toward the following business capabilities. • All the business capabilities that has impact on business services that has requirements to send the bulk data through files • Enterprise Technology Planning and Cost-effective Operation (e.g. MFT platform Selection) Refer to business capability document in the reference section for detailed explanation on each capability.
Architectural Observations	The following observation has identified the need for Security Platform solution. • File transfer related pain points

5.3.33 Service Governance Using Registry and Repository

Table 5.73 describes the SOA Service Governance and its importance.

5.3.34 Other Frameworks

There are other frameworks (e.g. Content, Batch, XML, SOAP, Testing, IDEs) which are not elaborated in this version can be detailed in the subsequent versions based on specific requirements of foundation services.

TABLE 5.73

SOA Service Governance

Overview	Enterprise Service Governance framework is a solution that provides design and runtime platform for managing service interfaces. Enterprise Service Governance framework is defined as part of foundation services in the Enterprise Architecture to provide service governance standards & guidelines, design and runtime governance solution using registry and repository. Service Governance framework can evolve as described below.
	• Define service standards & guidelines, design & runtime governance solution using registry and repository • Extend the Service Registry and Repository product framework based on specific requirements of service governance and enhance standards and guidelines with potential reusable governance services for the applications to reuse in their architecture
Need	Enterprise Service Governance Framework is needed to:
	• Avoid duplicate development of services for the same functionality • Avoid multiple custom service governance solutions are being built • Enable Standardization of Service Design and Runtime Discovery and Reuse • Adopt emerging technology in the Service Governance implementation • Improved separation of concerns between Service Execution and Management • Reusable Service Governance services (e.g. Inquire Service Existence, Check Service Availability, Get Service Policy) • Service Governance Technology standardization
Enabling Technology Capabilities	Enterprise Service Governance platform needs to have the following key IT enablers (but not limited to) thus enabling business capabilities to achieve strategic objectives.
	• Service metadata management—create or reuse service descriptions, taxonomies, XML Schemas and other service metadata artifacts • Design time Reuse—Enables to locate the required service interface during design • Service Publishing—Publish the service specification during deployment with customized descriptions • Service Interaction—Able to access service meta data and end point information including capturing of service metrics to assess performance • Support for WSDL, XML, XSD, BPEL, SCA and other standards • Integrated workflow for service governance • Administration interface (access control, policy changes etc.) • UDDI Support and Security

(Continued)

TABLE 5.73

(Continued)

Traceability Principles	The following set of Architecture Principles needs to be enforced from the platform selection through strategy to implementation.
	• **Prefer Use over Buy over Build**
	• **Drive for Reusable Solution Building Blocks**
	• **Base Architecture on Service Orientation**
	• **Comply to Standards**
	• **Rationalize Technology**
	• **Secure Information**
	• **Reduce Manual Interventions**
Business Capability	The Enterprise Service Governance Framework as part of foundation services is defined to contribute toward the following business capabilities.
	• All other business capabilities which has impact to business processes that leverage process, business, application and integration and data services
	• Enterprise Technology Planning and Cost-effective Operation (e.g. Service Governance Solution Selection)
Architectural Observations	The following observation has identified the need for the Logging and Auditing Platform solution.
	• Need for Common Integration Services
	• Need for Service Interface governance
	• Technology Standardization
	• Emerging Technology Adoption

5.3.35 Other Foundation Technology Services

There are additional foundation technology services that have also been included based on our previous experience but not elaborated in detail, including:

- Configuration service
- Cross reference service
- Visibility service

5.3.36 Other Foundation Platform Services

- Communications
  o Email services
  o Media/multimedia
  o Conferencing
- Reporting and analytics
  o Predictive analytics
  o Performance analysis and metrics
- Integration
  o Product Engineering
- Information
  o MDM services
  o Product services
  o Customer support services
  o Data management
  o Content management
- Governance
  o Authorization registry/repository
- Security
  o VPN
  o Firewall management
- Operations
  o Issue management

5.3.37 Solution Building Blocks Options: PSM

Solution Building Blocks (SBB) are candidate solution options to realize the ABBs present in the Enterprise Architecture. Solution Options for Technology functions:

  o Application server
  o Web server
  o Portal
  o BPM
  o Integration platform

- Solution options for foundation services

   o Frameworks

   o Technology services

   o Foundation platform services

As part of the product selection/evaluation, some of the general representative parameters that can be used for evaluation can include the following in Table 5.74.

The solution options listed in the following sections are illustrative based on factors like:

   o Leading analyst reports

   o Industry trends

   o Alignment with ABBs

It is duly noted that the intention below is *not* to make recommendations on any solution option as that will take deeper analysis of specific requirements and necessary due diligence and analysis. The following section is intended to provide some indicative options.

TABLE 5.74

Product Selection/Evaluation Criteria

General Criteria	Description
Market Presence	Revenue, customer base, no. years, roadmap
TCO	Cost of license, infrastructure
Architecture and Technology Support	J2EE/.NET, SOA, cloud-enabled, SaaS-ready, SOA support, Web 2.0, multi-lingual, integration, security etc.
Standards and Compliance	e.g. regulatory, financial,technology standards
Reference Case Studies	Implementation of case studies in the similar industry
Vendor Experience	Preferred vendor experience in the product
Industry Analyst Recommendation	Leading analyst recommendation (e.g. Magic Quadrant)
Functionality/Capability Mapping	Functional requirements or use cases mapping
Professional Services Support	SLA for critical issues, maintenance support model
Legacy System Integration	Pre-built adapters, legacy protocol support for transition
Architecture Principles Alignment	Alignment to Architecture Principles (related to general election, e.g. **Prefer Use over Buy over Build** as well as solution area, e.g. **Secure Information**)
Envisioned Future State Enterprise Architecture Alignment	Ability to expose and consume services in alignment with the Architecture Building Blocks (e.g. a CRM system exposing customer care services for say consumption by the orchestration or portal/view layer and consuming customer data view services) Ability to trigger other ABB services at right events (e.g. invoking an MDM service appropriately to update an enterprise entity near real-time in alignment with Architecture Principle **Maintain Gold Copy of Data**)

5.3.38 Technology Functions

5.3.38.1 Application Servers

Modern application servers act as foundation platform for deployment of presentation/ portal services, process orchestration services, business services, integration services, foundation services and application & data services.

Based on Architecture Principle on standards (**Comply to Standards**), it is recommended to have catalog of standard application server/s to bring consistency and technology sustainability.

The following points are in alignment with Architecture Principle: **Prefer Use over Buy over Build**:

- Use COTS application server for each Technology (e.g. JEE,.NET, PHP) for highly scalable and support critical solution
- Use Open Source Standard application server for each Technology (e.g. JEE,.NET, PHP) for licensing cost considerations

Table 5.75 provides the list of SBBs that comprises of COTS and Open source solutions to implement application server (Table 5.76).

TABLE 5.75

SBBs for Application Server

Technology	Key Products	Considerations

Java/JEE	• COTS
	  • IBM WebSphere Application Server
	  • Oracle WebLogic Application Server
	  • SAP NetWeaver Application Server
	• Open Source
	  • Apache Geronimo
	  • Glassfish
	  • JBOSS
	  • Tomcat (only for Web container)
		• WebSphere and WebLogicapplication servers are comprehensive platforms
		• SAP NetWeaver can claim attention (but not necessarily be an obvious selection) if SAP is selected as the ERP solution
		• JBOSS can be considered for lower licensing cost and a good one within Open Source options coming with modules on messaging, cache, etc.

.Net	• COTS
	  • IIS
	  • NET Framework (Windows Communication Foundation, Web Services,.NET Remoting, MSMQ, ASP.NET, ADO.NET)
	  • Share Point Portal for Presentation
	• Open Source
	  • TNAPS
		• Share point portal with IIS and .NET Framework combination can be potential application server platform for presentation layer
		• TNAPS .NET application server is cost-effective solution for .NET components and can also be deployed on Cloud platform like Amazon EC2 etc.

PHP	• COTS
	  • Zend Server
	• Open Source
	  • Zend Server Community Edition
		• With PHP solutions in the existing technology stack, Zend Server can be leveraged for business-critical PHP applications
		• Zend server can also be deployed on Cloud platform (like Amazon EC2) to minimize the utilization cost

TABLE 5.76

Considerations for Application Server Selection

Synopsis/Summary	
Considerations	The following could be potential considerations during product selection and implementation: • WebSphere, WebLogic stand-out as two of the industry leading, comprehensive application servers from the java world • COTS application server for each Technology (e.g. JEE, .NET, PHP) can be included in the technology catalog for highly scalable and support critical solution • Open Source Standard application server for each Technology (e.g. JEE , .NET, PHP) can be included in the technology catalog for (cost-effective solution) licensing cost consideration • ERP Strategy may have impact on the choice of standard application server stack

5.3.38.2 Web Servers

Modern Web servers act as foundation platform for deployment of presentation services that include HTML, Web 2.0 components, images, scripts and style sheets.

Based on Architecture Principle on Technology Rationalization (**Rationalize Technology**), it is recommended to have catalog of standard web server/s to bring consistency and technology sustainability.

Aligning with the Architecture Principle: **Prefer Use over Buy over Build**, the following points can be considered:

• COTS web server for each Technology (e.g. JEE, .NET, PHP) for highly scalable and support critical solution
• Open Source Standard WEB server for each Technology (e.g.JEE, .NET, PHP) for licensing cost considerations

Table 5.77 lists illustrative SBBs (across COTS and Open Source options) for Web Server solutions (Table 5.78).

TABLE 5.77

SBBs for Web Servers

Technology	Key Products	Considerations

Java/JEE	• COTS
	  • IBM HTTP Server
	  • Oracle HTTP Server
	• Open Source
	  • Apache HTTP Server
	  • JBoss Web Server
	  • Jetty
	  • Tomcat HTTP Server
		• IBM and Oracle HTTP Servers are bundled with respective application server package and has comprehensive features
		• JBOSS Web Server
		  • Licensing cost-effective
		  • Provides benefit of bundled Apache (integration) and Tomcat
		  • Complementary modules (PHP, URL Rewrite)

.NET	• COTS
	  • IIS Server
	• Open Source
	  • NA
		• NA

TABLE 5.78

Standardization of Web Server Considerations

Synopsis/Summary	
Considerations	The following could be potential considerations during standardization of web servers: • Standardization of application server will have impact on the Web Servers as both are mostly bundled together • Existing Apache and Tomcat web server installations as part of current state may have a bearing on the choice • Oracle and IBM are two of the leading products in the Portal space for a java ecosystem • ERP Strategy may have impact on the choice of standard web server stack

5.3.38.3 Portal

5.3.38.3.1 Portal Solution

Table 5.79 provides the list of SBBs (across COTS, Open Source options) for Portal solution (Table 5.80).

TABLE 5.79

SBBs for Portal Solution

Technology	Key Products	Considerations

Java/JEE	• COTS
	  • Back base
	  • IBM WebSphere Portal
	  • Oracle WebLogic Portal
	  • SAP NetWeaver Portal
	• Open Source
	  • JBOSS Enterprise Portal Platform
	  • Liferay Portal
		• IBM WebSphere & Oracle Portal Servers are
		  • Comprehensive Portal Platforms for complex and transaction-based UI solutions
		  • Large customer base
		  • Professional Support
		  • Higher TCO due to overall cost of Portal and its dependent products (WebSphere & WebLogic application server)
		  • Oracle WebLogic gets additional consideration in case Oracle ERP is selected.
		• SAP NetWeaver Portal gets more into consideration in case ERP is SAP solution
		• Liferay Portal is part of leader in the magic quadrant and has strong customer base
		• JBOSS Enterprise Portal complements with open source application server, ESB and messaging platform

.NET	• COTS
	  • Microsoft Share Point
	• Open Source
	  • NA
		• Microsoft Share Point portal can be more attractive as a choice for corporate intranet solutions.

TABLE 5.80

Considerations during Portal Selection

Synopsis/Summary	

Considerations	The following could be potential considerations during portal standardization:
	
	• Liferay Portal/JBOSS Enterprise Portal could be potential open source solution for horizontal portals to lower TCO
	• Microsoft Share Point can be potential solution to leverage existing share point environment
	• Based on ERP strategy, the portal platform product selection may have a high impact as ERP solution is bundled with portal solutions as well (e.g. SAP—NetWeaver Portal, Oracle—Web Logic Portal)
	• IBM or Oracle products can be selected as comprehensive and industry leading offerings for a java ecosystem
	• Additional High-level criteria for product selection
	  • Portal capabilities listed in PIM section
	  • ERP Strategy
	  • Portal Requirements

5.3.38.3.2 eCommerce

Table 5.81 lists illustrative SBBs (across COTS and Open Source options) for eCommerce solutions (Table 5.82).

5.3.38.4 Integration

5.3.38.4.1 ESB

Table 5.83 lists illustrative SBBs (across COTS and Open Source options) for Integration Platform (Table 5.84).

TABLE 5.81

SBBs for eCommerce Solution

Technology	Key Products

JEE/.NET	• COTS
	  • ATG
	  • Hybris
	  • IBM WebSphere
	  • Oracle iStore
	
	• Open Source
	  • Magento

TABLE 5.82

Considerations during eCommerce Product Selection

Synopsis/Summary	

Considerations	The following could be potential considerations during product selection and implementation
	• Additional high-level criteria for product selection
	  • eCommerce capabilities listed in PIM section
	  • ERP Strategy
	  • Portal selection
	  • eCommerce requirements

TABLE 5.83

Integration Platform SBBs

Technology	Key Products	Considerations

Java/JEE	• COTS
	  • IBM WebSphere ESB
	  • Oracle Service Bus (OSB)
	  • SAP NetWeaver
	  • TIBCO EMS
	• Open Source
	  • Mule ESB
	  • ServiceMix
	  • WS02
		• WebSphere ESB suite has multiple flavors, viz. Base ESB, Advanced ESB, Message Broker. It needs highly-priced WAS platform as runtime
		• Oracle Service Bus is the specialized ESB offering from Oracle (there is a mediation component that comes as part of Oracle SOA Suite bundle as well)
		• TIBCO EMS plays niche role in the integration space as it stands neutral platform between IBM, Oracle and MS
		• SAP NetWeaver get more consideration if SAP ERP is chosen
		• WSO2, ServiceMix, Mule can be considered for its licensing cost
		• WSO2 ESB is has comprehensive support and present in the leader category of leading analyst report

.Net	• COTS
	  • Microsoft BizTalk Server
	• Open Source
	  • NA
		• BizTalk supports only .Net and windows platform but can interoperate with Java through web services

TABLE 5.84

Considerations for Integration Platform Selection

Synopsis/Summary	
Considerations	The following could be potential considerations during ESB or Integration platform technology standardizations • IBM and Oracle products come into strong consideration for a java ecosystem • Based on ERP strategy, the ESB platform product selection may have an impact since ERP solution comes with ESB platform as well (SAP—NetWeaver ESB, Oracle—OSB) • As most of the COTS ESB has similar capabilities, the selection may depend on additional criteria. • language platform, future roadmap of product, integration with legacy, cloud friendly, hosted service

5.3.38.5 Process Orchestration

5.3.38.5.1 BPM

Table 5.85 lists illustrative SBBs (across COTS and Open Source options) for BPM Platform (Table 5.86).

TABLE 5.85

SBBs for BPM Platform

Technology	Key Products	Considerations

Java/JEE	• COTS
	  • Appian Enterprise
	  • IBM WebSphere BPM Suite (Process Modeler, Process Server)
	  • Oracle BPM Suite, BPA
	  • Pega Systems
	  • SAP NetWeaver BPM and BRMS Software AG—WebMethods
		• Comprehensive BPM platform for complex and transaction-based UI solutions
		• Large customer base
		• Professional support
		• Stable and scalable platform
		• Higher TCO in terms of cost of base product and its dependent products

	• Open Source
	  • Intalio
	  • JBPM
		• Intalio
		  • Comprehensive BPM Platform
		  • Cloud friendly and has stable roadmap
		  • Supports BPMN
		  • Professional support
		• JBPM
		  • Licensing cost-effective solution for simple people or document workflows
		  • Custom user interface need to be developed for business user friendly task administration
		  • Support through email

.NET	• COTS
	  • Metastorm (OpenText) BPM
	• Open Source
	  • NA
		• Strengths
		  • Ease integration with MS Sharepoint, Windows Foundation, BizTalk, SQL Server and office products
		• Considerations
		  • Uses few proprietary modeling notations hence portability of BPEL may be low
		  • Metastorm was acquired by OpenText hence roadmap of Provision BPM product needs to be checked with new vendor
		  • Interoperability with Java platform to be considered
		  • Portability and Scalability may have some limitations due to .NET running on windows platform
		  • Version x has major revamp on their architecture

TABLE 5.86

Considerations for BPM Platform Selection

Synopsis/Summary	

Considerations	The following could be potential considerations during product selection and implementation
	
	• Since Metastorm BPM platform is present in analyst magic leader quadrant and already available, it can be considered as potential choice of Process Orchestration layer as a default option and assessed for implication against standards chosen for technology (e.g. java versus dot net) and others
	• Additional high-level criteria for product selection
	  • BPM capabilities listed in PIM section
	  • ERP strategy
	  • Performance requirements

5.3.39 Frameworks

5.3.39.1 UI Framework/s

Table 5.87 provides the list of COTS and Open Source products or frameworks in the user interface area (Table 5.88).

5.3.39.2 Application Framework/s

Table 5.89 lists illustrative SBBs (across COTS and Open Source options) for Application (AKA Business tier) Frameworks (Table 5.90).

TABLE 5.87

User Interface SBBs

Technology	Key Products

Java/JEE	• COTS
	  • NA
	
	• Open Source
	  • Spring MVC (Java)
	  • JSF (Java)
	  • Struts (Java)
	  • Tapestry

.NET	• COTS
	  • NA
	• Open Source
	  • Spring.Web (.NET)

TABLE 5.88

UI Product Selection Considerations

Synopsis/Summary	
Considerations	The following could be potential considerations during product selection and implementation: • Product selection of Application Server and Web Server need to considered for compatibility support of UI Frameworks • Based on ERP strategy, the UI framework selection may have an impact • Existing Spring MVC implementations in some of the applications may have a bearing on the choice

TABLE 5.89

SBBs for Application Frameworks

Technology	Key Products

Java/JEE	• COTS
	  • Product based container frameworks (JEE EJB)
	
	• Open Source
	  • Spring.Java

.NET	• COTS
	  • Product based container frameworks (.NET)
	• Open Source
	  • Spring.Net

TABLE 5.90

Considerations for Applications Framework Selection

Synopsis/Summary	

Considerations	The following could be potential considerations during product selection and implementation
	
	• Application server need to be considered while selecting frameworks for compatibility support
	• Application frameworks can be standardized based on
	  • Application Server catalog
	  • Framework requirements
	  • Integration Support with Web Tier or UI frameworks

5.3.39.3 ORM Framework/s

Table 5.91 lists illustrative SBBs (across COTS and Open Source options) for data access layer leveraging Object Relational Mapping (ORM) (Table 5.92).

5.3.39.4 Cache Framework/s

Table 5.93 lists illustrative SBBs (across COTS and Open Source options) for Cache Management solution (Table 5.94).

TABLE 5.91

Data Access Layer SBBs

Technology	Key Products

Java/JEE	• COTS
	  • Oracle—TOPLINK
	
	• Open Source
	  • Hibernate for Java
	  • myBATIS

.NET	• COTS
	  • ADO.NET Entity Framework
	• Open Source
	  • nHibernate for .NET

TABLE 5.92

Product Selection Considerations for ORM Framework

Synopsis/Summary	

Considerations	The following could be potential considerations during product selection and implementation:
	
	• Hibernate or MyBATIS are compatible with most of the application servers
	• ADO.NET Entity framework is part of Biztalk and share point portal server technologies
	• TOPLINK works well with Oracle SOA suite
	• Additional high-level criteria for selection may include
	  • Application Server catalog
	  • Batch container support
	  • Integration Support with Business tier frameworks
	  • Data access layer requirements

TABLE 5.93

Cache Management SBBs

Technology	Key Products

JEE/.NET	• COTS
	   • NCache Express (Free)
	   • Oracle Coherence
	   • TerraCotta—Enterprise EHCache
	• Open Source
	   • EHCache (Open Source)
	   • JBoss Cache
	   • OSCache

TABLE 5.94

Considerations for Cache Management Product Selection

Synopsis/Summary	

Considerations	The following could be potential considerations during product selection and implementation:
	
	• JBOSS Cache is logical choice for JBOSS Enterprise application server
	• OS Cache/EHCache are application server agnostic implementations
	• Enterprise EHCache is having professional support from Terracotta
	• The high-level criteria for selection may include
	   • Cache applicability requirements
	   • Choice of application server and language
	   • Integration support with UI, business tier, ORM frameworks
	   • Professional support
	   • Cost

5.3.40 Foundation Platforms

5.3.40.1 Mobile Services

Table 5.95 lists illustrative SBBs (across COTS and Open Source options) for Mobile Services solution (Table 5.96).

TABLE 5.95

Mobile Services SBBs

Technology	Key Products	Considerations

JEE/.NET	• COTS
	   • Antenna
	   • Apple
	   • IBM
	   • Microsoft
	   • RIM
	   • SAP Spring Wireless
	   • Syclo
	• Open Source
	   • Rhomobilie
		• Antenna, SAP and Syclo has the cross-OS development platform support hence one programming can be leveraged for multiple OS (iPhone, Android, Windows, Symbhion etc.)
		• Spring Wireless is used only for Mobile web client applications hence do not have app development support
		
		• Rhomobilie
		   • Has open source cross platform support
		   • Has integration server to reduce coding for backend integration
		   • Has SaaS model for integration server

TABLE 5.96

Considerations for Mobile Services Strategy

Synopsis/Summary	
Considerations	The following could be potential considerations during Mobile Services Strategy: • Mobile Services Technology Capabilities listed in PIM section • Portal or Application Server Support for mobile delivery • Cross platform support and standards support

5.3.40.2 IVR Services

Table 5.97 lists illustrative SBBs (across COTS and Open Source options) for IVR solutions (Table 5.98).

5.3.40.3 FAX Integration

Table 5.99 provides the list of SBBs that comprise of COTS and open source products (or) frameworks to implement FAX Integration (Table 5.100).

TABLE 5.97

IVR Services SBBs

Technology	Key Products

JEE/.NET	• COTS
	    • Avaya, Genesys, Nortel, Parlance
	    • CISCO IP Interactive Voice Response 8.0
	    • Intervoice, IBM, Microsoft
	    • Leverage CRM Product capabilities
	• Open Source
	    • NA

TABLE 5.98

IVR Product Selection Considerations

Synopsis/Summary	
Considerations	The following could be potential considerations during product selection and implementation • Enterprise IVR Business requirements

TABLE 5.99

Fax Integration SBBs

Technology	Key Products

JEE/.NET	• COTS
	    • OpenText—RightFax
	• Open Source
	    • Hylafax

TABLE 5.100

Considerations for Fax Integration Product Selection

Synopsis/Summary	
Considerations	The following could be potential considerations during product selection and implementation: • HylaFax solution can be considered for licensing cost-effective solution • Fax Service technology capabilities listed in PIM section considered for future state solution • Perform proof of technology on the selected product to avoid any unknown issues • FAX Integration business requirements

5.3.40.4 Web 2.0

Table 5.101 lists illustrative SBBs (across COTS and Open Source options) for Web 2.0 (Table 5.102).

TABLE 5.101

Web 2.0 SBBs

Technology	Key Products

JEE/.NET	• COTS
	   • Adobe Flex Builder (Development)
	
	• Open Source
	   • RIA—Flex
	      ■ Adobe Flex SDK
	      ■ Cairnogram
	      ■ Flex MVC
	      ■ MATE
	      ■ Swiz
	   • Flex Java
	      ■ BlazeDS
	   • RIA—AJAX Frameworks
	      ■ ASP.NET AJAX
	      ■ DOJO
	      ■ DWR
	      ■ GWT
	      ■ ICEFaces
	      ■ JQuery
	      ■ Spry (Open Source from Adobe)
	      ■ Yahoo UI
	   • Social Networking
	      ■ Blog—Pebble
	      ■ Chat—Claros
	      ■ RSS—Rome
	      ■ Wiki—JamWiki

TABLE 5.102

Considerations for Web 2.0 Product Selection

Snopsis/Summary	

Considerations	The following could be potential considerations during product selection and implementation:
	
	• Combination of frameworks and products listed above need to be considered for Web 2.0 solution
	• Additional high-level criteria of product selection
	   • Web 2.0 capabilities listed in the PIM section
	   • Enterprise Web 2.0 requirements

5.3.40.5 Reporting

Table 5.103 lists illustrative SBBs (across COTS and Open Source options) for Enterprise Reporting solution:

Table 5.104 describes the high-level summary of products (or) frameworks.

5.3.40.6 Business Activity Monitoring

Table 5.105 lists illustrative SBBs (across COTS and Open Source options) for BAM area (Table 5.106).

TABLE 5.103

Enterprise Reporting SBBs

Technology	Key Products

JEE/.NET	• COTS
	  • Actuate
	  • IBM Cognos
	  • Oracle Reports
	  • SAP Business Objects
	• Open Source
	  • JasperSoft

TABLE 5.104

Considerations for Enterprise Reporting Product Selection

Synopsis/Summary	

Considerations	The following could be potential considerations during product selection and implementation
	
	• JasperSoft is considered as licensing cost-effective solution and strong in the leading analyst ratings
	• JasperSoft is cloud friendly
	• IBM Cognos solution is potential consideration to leverage the existing investment (e.g. upgrade to latest version)
	• Additional High-level criteria of product selection
	  • Enterprise reporting requirements
	  • Reporting capabilities listed in the PIM section

TABLE 5.105

BAM SBBs

Technology	Key Products

JEE/.NET	• COTS
	  • IBM WebSphere BAM
	  • Microsoft BizTalk server BAM
	  • Oracle BAM
	  • Systar
	• Open Source
	  • WSO2

TABLE 5.106

Considerations for BAM Product Selection

Synopsis/Summary	
Considerations	The following could be potential considerations during product selection and implementation
	• Systar solution is based on .NET platform and has in-memory processing for high volume
	• Oracle BAM is available in JEE platform and gets more consideration in case Oracle SOA Suite is chosen
	• WebSphere BAM platform needs WAS application server which may increase overall TCO
	• BAM Technology Capabilities listed in PIM section can be considered for future state BAM selection
	• Applicability BAM Platform may depend on Enterprise Real-time monitoring requirements

5.3.40.7 Business Analytics

Table 5.107 provides the list of SBBs comprises of COTS and open source solutions to implement business analytics (Table 5.108).

TABLE 5.107

Business Analytics SBBs

Technology	Key Products
Java/JEE	• COTS
	• IBM BI
	• Information builders
	• MicroStrategy
	• Oracle BI Platform
	• SAP BusinessObjects
	• SAS
	• Open Source
	• JasperSoft
	• Pentaho
.NET	• COTS
	• Microsoft BI Platform
	• Open Source
	• NA

TABLE 5.108

Considerations for business analytics Product Selection

Snopsis/Summary	
Considerations	The following could be potential considerations during product selection and implementation
	• High-level influencing factors for solution selection
	• Business Analytics capabilities listed in the PIM section
	• Enterprise business analytics future state requirements
	• Existing Business analytical solutions (e.g. Oracle and Cognos)

5.3.40.8 Web Analytics

Table 5.109 lists illustrative SBBs (across COTS and Open Source options) for Web Analytics (Table 5.110).

5.3.40.9 File Transfer Management

Table 5.111 lists illustrative SBBs (across COTS and Open Source options) for Automated File Transfer Management (Table 5.112).

TABLE 5.109

Web Analytics SBBs

Technology	Key Products

Java/JEE	• COTS
	  • Coremetrics
	  • NedStat Omniture
	  • WebTrends
	
	• Open Source
	  • Google Analytics
	  • Open Web Analytics (OWA) (PHP Based)

.NET	• COTS
	  • Microsoft Share point Server—Web Analytics Capability
	• Open Source
	  • Open Web Analytics (OWA) (PHP Based)

TABLE 5.110

Considerations for Web Analytics Product Selection

Synopsis/Summary	

Considerations	The following could be potential considerations during product selection and implementation
	
	• Additional high-level influencing factors for solution selection
	  • Web Analytics capabilities listed in the PIM section
	  • Enterprise Web Analytics requirements
	  • Existing Web analytical solutions (e.g. Omniture, Google Analytics)

TABLE 5.111

Automated File Transfer SBBs

Technology	Key Products

JEE/.NET	• COTS
	  • Global Scape MFT (Cloud Friendly)
	  • Sterling MFT
	  • TIBCO MFT
	
	• Open Source
	  • NA

TABLE 5.112

Considerations for Automated File Transfer Product Selection

Synopsis/Summary	

Considerations	The following could be potential considerations during product selection and implementation:
	
	• High-level criteria for product selection can be
	   • Managed File transfer Capabilities listed in PIM section
	   • ERP Strategy
	   • SOA Suite

5.3.40.10 Enterprise Search

Table 5.113 provides the list of SBBs comprises of COTS and open source solutions to implement enterprise search functionality (Table 5.114).

TABLE 5.113

Enterprise Search SBBs

Technology	Key Products

JEE/.NET	• COTS
	   • EMC
	   • Endeca
	   • Microsoft Search
	   • IBM Search Product (OmniFind™ Enterprise Edition)
	   • Open Text
	   • Oracle Secure Enterprise Search
	
	• Open Source
	   • Apache Lucene
	   • Apache Solr
	   • SearchBlox (built on Apache Lucene)

TABLE 5.114

Considerations for Enterprise Search Product Selection

Synopsis/Summary	

Considerations	The following could be potential considerations during product selection and implementation
	
	• High-level criteria for product selection
	   • Search technology capabilities listed in PIM section
	   • Application integration support
	   • Portal solution dependency
	   • Enterprise search requirements
	   • Existing search solution (e.g. Lucene)

5.3.40.11 Security

Table 5.115 lists illustrative SBBs (across COTS and Open Source options) for security (Table 5.116).

5.3.41 Technology Services

5.3.41.1 Exception Management

Table 5.117 lists illustrative SBBs (across COTS and Open Source options) for centralized Exception Management (Table 5.118).

TABLE 5.115

Security SBBs

Technology	Key Products
JEE/.NET	<ul><li>COTS<ul><li>CA Technologies (Identity Manager, SiteMinder)</li><li>Entrust (Digital Security)</li><li>IBM—Tivoli suite</li><li>Oracle Identity Management Suite, Oracle Web Service Manager</li></ul></li><li>Open Source<ul><li>NA</li></ul></li></ul>

TABLE 5.116

Considerations for Security Product Selection

Synopsis/Summary	
Considerations	The following could be potential considerations during product selection and implementation <ul><li>Existing security solutions could be enhanced based on security requirements</li><li>Security solution capabilities listed in PIM section can be considered for future state solution</li><li>The high-level influencing factors for product selection can be<ul><li>SOA Suite selection</li></ul></li></ul>

TABLE 5.117

Exception Management SBBs

Technology	Key Products
JEE/.NET	<ul><li>Custom Built<ul><li>Reusable Exception Management base line framework</li><li>Centralized Exception Management Console</li></ul></li><li>Open Source<ul><li>NA</li></ul></li></ul>

TABLE 5.118

Considerations for Exception Management Product Selection

Synopsis./Summary	
Considerations	The following could be potential considerations during product selection and implementation • Exception management technology capabilities listed in PIM section • Enterprise exception management requirements

5.3.41.2 Enterprise Logging and Auditing

Table 5.119 lists illustrative SBBs (across COTS and Open Source options) for Centralized Enterprise Logging & Auditing Solution (Table 5.120).

5.3.41.3 Notification Service

Table 5.121 lists illustrative SBBs (across COTS and Open Source options) for centralized Notification Service solution (Table 5.122).

TABLE 5.119

Enterprise Logging and Auditing SBBs

Technology	Key Products

Java/JEE	• COTS
	  • NA
	
	• Open Source
	  • Log4j with Custom wrapper (e.g. JMS, MQ, WebService Appender)

.NET	• COTS
	  • Microsoft Enterprise Library Logging
	• Open Source
	  • Log4Net with Custom wrappers (e.g. JMS, MQ, WebService Appenders)

TABLE 5.120

Considerations for Enterprise Logging and Auditing Product Solution

Synopsis/Summary	

Considerations	The following could be potential considerations during product selection and implementation:
	
	• Enterprise logging and uditing requirements
	• Products has its own logging mechanism
	• Logging service evolution
	  • Standards with framework
	  • Customized reusable library with Log4j and Log4Net
	  • Centralized logging service with runtime infrastructure

TABLE 5.121

Notification Service SBBs

Technology	Key Products

JEE/.NET	• Custom built
	   • Custom service wrappers with open standard frameworks (Java Email, SMS Utilities)
	   • Leverage product (e.g. ERP, Application Server) capabilities
	• Open Source
	   • NA

TABLE 5.122

Considerations for Notification Service Product Selection

Synopsis/Summary	
Considerations	The following could be potential considerations during product selection and implementation: • Enterprise notification requirements • Out-of-the-box products' notification functionality • Notification capabilities listed in PIM section Custom solution that can be extended to support multiple channels

5.3.41.4 Rules Management Service

Table 5.123 lists illustrative SBBs (across COTS and Open Source options) for Business Rule Management System (BRMS) (Table 5.124).

TABLE 5.123

Business Rule Management System (BRMS) SBBs

Technology	Key Products

JEE/.NET	• COTS
	   • Corticon (BRMS—Java)
	   • FICO Blaze Advisor Enterprise Edition (BRMS—Java)
	   • IBM—WebSphere ILOG (BRMS—Java)
	
	• Open Source
	   • DROOLS (BRE Only—Java)
	   • JBOSS (BRMS—Java)
	   • NxBRE (BRE Only for .NET)
	   • OpenL Tablets (BRMS—Java)

TABLE 5.124

Considerations for BRMS Product Selection

Synopsis/Summary	

Considerations	The following could be potential considerations during product selection and implementation:
	
	• OpenL Tablets is cost-effective end-to-end solution
	• DROOLS provides only business rules engine and custom development needed for RULES management functionality
	• High-level criteria for product selection
	   • Rules management capabilities listed in PIM section
	   • Application integration support
	   • BPM solution may have in-built business rules engine

5.3.41.5 Scheduler Services

Table 5.125 lists illustrative SBBs (across COTS and Open Source options) for Scheduler functionality (Table 5.126).

5.3.41.6 Service Governance: SOA Registry

Table 5.127 lists illustrative SBBs (across COTS and Open Source options) for Service Governance (Table 5.128).

TABLE 5.125

Scheduler Services SBBs

Technology	Key Products

JEE/.NET	• COTS
	   • CA—AUTOSYS
	   • UC4 Automation Engine
	
	• Open Source
	   • Apache—Quartz.NET
	   • Terracotta—Quartz.Java

TABLE 5.126

Considerations for Scheduler Services Product Selection

Synopsis/Summary	
Considerations	The following could be potential considerations during product selection and implementation • Quartz.Java/.NET is a licensing cost-effective solution and strong open source platform scheduler. • Terracotta—Quartz.Java is built on top of Quartz engine to make it as enterprise class scheduler. • Scheduler technology capabilities listed in PIM section. • Enterprise scheduling requirements.

TABLE 5.127

SOA Governance SBBs

Technology	Key Products

JEE/.NET	• COTS
	   • AmberPoint (Oracle)
	   • IBM WSRR
	   • Oracle Service Registry
	   • SAP
	   • Software AG
	
	• Open Source
	   • WSO2

TABLE 5.128

Considerations for SOA Registry and Repository Product Selection

Synopsis/Summary	
Considerations	The following could be potential considerations during product selection and implementation:

- Software AG can work with multi-vendor application server (e.g. IBM, Oracle)
- Service registry and repository is dependent on SOA suite or ERP strategy. For example, Oracle Service Registry is a logical choice for Oracle SOA suite; AmberPoint works well with the rest of the Oracle stack, as well as other stacks as a leading product
- WSO2—In addition to registry and licensing cost-effectiveness, it has comprehensive SOA stack (e.g. application server, ESB, process server)
- Service governance technology capabilities listed in PIM section considered for future state solution
- Major drivers of product selection
  - Service governance future state requirements
  - SOA Suite dependency

5.3.42 Architectural Perspective of Selected Functional Areas

In this section, selected scenarios for key business functional areas (aka business functions areas) are presented to walkthrough the envisioned architecture. The objective is to help understand the architecture envisioned, in context of specific business scenarios, and see how the different architecture building blocks play specific roles to help realize such scenarios.

The primary focus of this section is to capture the reference building blocks with interaction of business scenarios presented during technology workshops which would provide architectural inputs for the individual programs or projects identified in the roadmap aligned to functional areas.

1. Order Management
2. Procurement and Vendor Management
3. Rights and Royalties
4. Financial Management
5. Dynamic Content Management
6. CRM and Sales
7. Product Management
8. BI and Reporting

5.3.43 Order Management

In this section, Order Management functional area is elaborated with key influencing factors, candidate business scenario.

5.3.43.1 Influencing Factors

Based on the current state observations, business capabilities and architecture principles, the following are the key influencing factors (but not limited to) that may drive directly or indirectly order management solution implementation (Table 5.129).

TABLE 5.129

Order Management Influencing Factors

Key Influencing factors

• **Unified Portal for Order Management**
   • **One-stop portal for order management that would encompass shopping cart, order tracking, fulfillment, returns and warehouse user interface functions.**
• **Multi-Channel Support Order Entry**
   • **Orders through other channels such as mobileemail, EDI, Tablets etc.**
• **Adopting to Service Oriented Architecture**
   • **SOA strategy and architecture design principles**
• **Foundation Services**
   • **Availability of framework/shared services to promote reusability and standards**
• **Enterprise Integration Platform**
   • **Foundational platform required for solving integration issues**
• **Enterprise Application Integration Services**
   • **Order Management integration with CRM, finance, inventory, royalties through integration platform using real-time, near real-time or batch mode**
   • **Integration with legacy systems during transition phase**
• **Technology Standardization**
   • **Technology standards and best practices related to Order Management solution**
• **Data Standardization**
   • **Standard canonicals for key business entities (Product, Order, Customer, Partner, Vendor, Price etc.) that Order Management solution leverages**
• **Application rationalization—global order management solution**
   • **Consolidation of geo-specific and product specific functionalities to support global solution.**
• **Infrastructure Strategy**
   • **Strategy toward infrastructure capabilities such as hosting, cloud computing and virtualization which in turn would drive the Order Management product solution**

Table 5.130 provides the responsibility of each step with brief description:

TABLE 5.130

Order Management Candidate Business Scenario

Step	Description
1.	Customer calls support team through IVR channel for placing the order through phone
2.	Customer Support Representative (CSR) attends the call and logs into portal to initiate the process
3.	Order Management business process is initiated from the portal
4.	Depending on the entry point of the business process, CSR gets the Order capture view
5.	CSR captures the customer and product information and Order quantity details. CRM & Sales and Product Management business functions are leveraged
6.	Product inventory and Price is checked for availability and blocked for purchase. Inventory management and Price& Discounts business functions are leveraged
7.	CSR captures the payment details and sends the credit card details for validation through common external service integration platform
8.	Invoice is prepared and sends it to the customer
9.	Account receivables are sent to Finance business function for collecting the payment
10.	Depending on the fulfillment options, the order is fulfilled through digital distribution, physical distribution or 3rd party fulfillment through integration platform

5.3.44 Procurement & Vendor Management

In this section, Procurement & Vendor Management functional area is elaborated with key influencing factors, candidate business scenario.

5.3.44.1 Influencing Factors

Based on the current state observations, business capabilities and architecture principles, the following are the key influencing factors (but not limited to) that may drive directly or indirectly Global Procurement and Vendor Management solution implementation (Table 5.131).

TABLE 5.131

Procurement & Vendor Management Influencing Factors

Key Influencing factors

• Unified Portal for Procurement and Vendor management
  • One-stop portal for Procurement and Vendor management that would encompass creation of service request tracking, procurement fulfillment, integrated view of supplier network and Vendor Management user interface functions.
• Multi-Channel Support Procurement Order Entry
  • Procurement orders or requests through channels such as Web, Mobile, Email, Tablets etc.
• Adopting to Service Oriented Architecture
  • SOA Strategy and Architecture design principles helps Procurement solution to be modular with separation of concerns
• Framework Services and Shared Services
  • Availability of framework/shared services to promote reusability and consistency
• Enterprise Integration Platform
  • Foundational platform required for solving integration issues with supplier/vendor systems
• Enterprise Application Integration Services
  • Procurement and Vendor solution integration with Finance, Legal and external systems viz. Vendors, Analyst feed etc.
  • Integration of legacy systems during transition phase
• Technology Standardization
  • Technology standards and best practices related to Procurement and Vendor Management solution
• Data Standardization
  • Standard canonicals for key business entities (Vendor, Partner, Contract, Terms, Price etc.) that Procurement and Vendor Management solution leverages.
• Application rationalization—Procurement and Vendor management current solution if present
  • Consolidation of geo-specific and product specific functionalities to support global procurement and vendor solution.
• Infrastructure Strategy
  • Strategy toward infrastructure capabilities such as hosting, cloud computing and virtualization which in turn would drive the Procurement and Vendor Management product solution

5.3.44.2 Procurement & Vendor Management: Business Scenarios

The following business scenarios are selected to represent the sequence of interaction steps within architecture building blocks:

- Procurement Service Request received from internal services
- Vendor is not available hence selection of vendor process is triggered
- Vendor is selected through RFP/RFI process
- New Vendor is created after signing the contract

TABLE 5.132

Procurement & Vendor Management Candidate Business Scenario

Step	Description
1.	Internal departments logging into the Procurement portal to place a purchase/procurement request
2.	Search for available vendors and products as part of vendor/product catalog
3.	Since there is no single vendor/product to fulfill the current need, user decides to initiate a service request process of procurement
4.	Service Request Process interacts with business functions to identify a new vendor for the procurement requested
5.	Initiates vendor selection process to create RFP/RFI and list of initial vendors
6.	Develop RFP/RFI through iterative process
7.	Get the analyst ratings through real-time integration with external sources who can provide analyst rating data for filtering out the vendors
8.	Share the RFP/RFI to the selected vendors through external integration (e.g. email services)
9.	Once the vendor is selected through iterative process then contract is prepared with the help of Legal business function
10.	Sign the contract with selected vendor and update the system with the signed contract
11.	Setup the vendor and create the definition of vendor in the Vendor data store through information services

Scenarios validation helps to identify and/or validate any missing building blocks from presentation, functional, integration and foundation building blocks perspective and also refine the responsibility of building blocks (Table 5.132).

5.3.45 Rights and Royalties Management

In this section, rightsand royalties functional area is elaborated with key influencing factors.

5.3.45.1 Influencing Factors

Based on the current state observations, business capabilities and architecture principles, the following are the key influencing factors (but not limited to) that may drive directly or indirectly Rights, Royalties and Permission solution implementation (Table 5.133).

TABLE 5.133

Rights and Royalties Management Influencing Factors

Key Influencing factors
• **Unified Portal for Rights and Royalties management**
• **Unified Portal solution for Rights Management (e.g. track acquisition and distribution), Royalty Management (e.g. royalty contracts, payment calculation), Permissions Management (e.g. Compliance tracking, permission definition, negotiation).**
• **Multi-Channel Support Royalty, Rights and Permission User interfaces**
• **Requests through channels such as web, mobile, email, tablets etc.**
• **Adopting to Service Oriented Architecture**
• **SOA Strategy and Architecture design principles helps Rights, Royalty and Permission solution to be modular with separation of concerns**

(Continued)

TABLE 5.133

(Continued)

Key Influencing factors

- Foundations Services
  - Availability of foundation services to promote reusability and standards
- Enterprise Integration Platform
  - Integration platform required for solving P2P integration issues with source (asset owners) systems
- Enterprise Application Integration Services
  - Rights and Royalties solution real-time integration with Finance, Legal and external systems viz. Source systems etc.
  - Legacy systems integration during transition phase
- Technology Standardization
  - Technology standards and best practices related to Rights, Royalties and Permissions Management solution
- Data Standardization
  - Standard canonicals for key business entities (e.g. rights, royalties, royalty contract, permission) that rights, royalties and permission solutions leverage.
- Application rationalization—rights, royalties and permission current solution if present
  - Consolidation of geo-specific and product specific functionalities to support global rights, royalties and permission solution.
- Infrastructure Strategy
  - Strategy toward infrastructure capabilities such as hosting, cloud computing and virtualization which in turn would drive the rights, royalties and permissions management product solution

5.3.46 Dynamic Content Management

In this section, Content Management functional area is elaborated with key influencing factors.

5.3.46.1 Influencing Factors

Table 5.134 include some of the key influencing factors that may drive directly or indirectly Dynamic Content Management solution.

TABLE 5.134

Dynamic Content Management Influencing Factors

Key Influencing factors

- Unified Portal for Dynamic Content management
  - Unified Portal solution for Content Authoring, QA, Administration and Production.
- Multi-Channel Support Content Management User interfaces
  - Content Acquisition and Delivery through channels such as Web, Mobile, Email, Tablets etc.
- Adopting to Service Oriented Architecture
  - SOA Strategy and Architecture design principles helps Content Management solution to be modular with separation of concerns
- Foundations Services
  - Availability of Foundation Services to promote reusability and standards
- Enterprise Integration Platform
  - Integration platform required for solving P2P integration issues with Content Providers (e.g. Authors, Vendors) and Consumers (e.g. Apple, Amazon, Distributors)

TABLE 5.134

(Continued)

Key Influencing factors

- Enterprise Application Integration Services
  - Content Management solution real-time, near real-time, batch integration with other business functions (e.g. Product Management, Permission Systems, Order Management)
  - Legacy systems integration during transition phase
- Technology Standardization
  - Technology standards and best practices related to Content Management solution
- Data Standardization
  - Standard canonicals for key business entities (e.g. Content Metadata, Asset, Component, Chapter) that Content Management solutions leverage.
- Application rationalization—Content Management Solution
  - Consolidation of geo-specific and product specific functionalities to support global Content Management solution.
- Infrastructure Strategy
  - Strategy toward infrastructure capabilities such as hosting, cloud computing and virtualization which in turn would drive the Content Management solution

5.3.47 CRM & Sales

In this section, CRM & Sales functional area is elaborated with key influencing factors, candidate business scenario.

5.3.47.1 Influencing Factors

Table 5.135 include some of the key representative influencing factors that may drive directly or indirectly CRM solution.

TABLE 5.135

CRM & Sales Influencing Factors

Key Influencing factors

- Unified Portal for CRM
  - Unified Portal solution for customer care, customer data management, customer analytics, sales management and loyalty.
- Multi-Channel Support CRM User interfaces
  - Customer care and customer interaction through channels such as web, mobile, chat, IVR, email, tablets etc.
- Adopting to Service Oriented Architecture
  - SOA strategy and architecture design principles helps CRM solution to be modular with separation of concerns
- Foundations Services
  - Availability of foundation services to promote reusability and stand ards
- Enterprise Integration Platform
  - Integration platform required for solving P2P integration issues with external sales channels (e.g. Amazon) and customer systems

(Continued)

TABLE 5.135

(Continued)

Key Influencing factors

- Enterprise Application Integration Services
  - CRM solution real-time, near real-time, batch integration with other business functions (e.g. Product Management, Rights and Royalties Management, Order Management, Pricing and Discounts, Marketing management, Finance management)
  - Legacy systems integration during transition phase
- Technology Standardization
  - Technology standards and best practices related to CRM solution
- Data Standardization
  - Standard canonicals for key business entities (e.g. customer, customer case, loyalty, customer activity, contract, contact) that CRM solutions leverage.
- Application rationalization—CRM Solution
  - Consolidation of geo-specific and product specific functionalities to support global CRM solution.
- Infrastructure Strategy
  - Strategy toward infrastructure capabilities such as hosting, cloud computing and virtualization which in turn would drive the CRM solution

5.3.47.2 CRM: Business Scenarios

The following business scenarios are selected to depict the sequence of interaction steps within architecture building blocks:

- Customer acquisition
- Contact center analytics
- Support ticket created through self-service portal and IVR channel

Scenarios validation helps to identify and/or validate any missing building blocks from presentation, process, business, and integration and foundation building blocks perspective, refine the responsibility of building blocks and alignment of fitness in the overall ecosystem (Table 5.136).

5.3.47.2.1 Customer Acquisition

TABLE 5.136

Customer Acquisition Candidate Business Scenario

1. Sales/Marketing identifies new customer segments through multiple forms of process
2. Customer acquisition business process is initiated through Sales view
3. Customer acquisition process leverages Sales management service's prospects business function to analyze the data
4. Prospecting services gathers information from various aspects like marketing info, Product info, similar Customer analytics and external data to develop influencing strategy
5. Sales and Marketing team develops product concept/proposal for marketing plan a) Align customer need with product and qualify opportunities. Iterate until proposal is approved
6. Approved proposal is shared with prospecting customer and gain agreement with customer
7. Sales role logs into Customer Management portal and setup customer contract & Customer data is created in CDM

5.3.48 Financial Management

In this section, Financial Management functional area is elaborated with key influencing factors, candidate business scenario.

5.3.48.1 Influencing Factors

Table 5.137 include some of the key influencing factors that may drive directly or indirectly Financial Management solution.

5.3.48.2 Finance: Business Scenario

The following business scenario is selected to represents the sequence of interaction steps within architecture building blocks:

- Vendor Payment

Scenarios validation helps to identify and/or validate any missing building blocks from presentation, process, business, and integration and foundation building blocks perspective, refine the responsibility of building blocks and alignment of fitness in the overall ecosystem (Table 5.138).

TABLE 5.137

Financial Management Influencing Factors

Key Influencing factors
• **Unified Portal for Financial management** • **Unified Portal solution for Accounting, A/R, A/P, Asset Management, Corporate Finance, Reporting and Planning & Analysis.** • **Multi-Channel Support Financial Management User interfaces** • **User interfaces (e.g. A/R, A/P, reporting) through channels such as web, mobile, email, tabletetc.** • **Adopting to Service-Oriented Architecture** • **SOA Strategy and Architecture design principles helps Finance Management solution to be modular with separation of concerns** • **Foundations Services** • **Availability of Foundation Services to promote reusability and standards** • **Enterprise Integration Platform** • **Integration platform required for solving P2P integration issues with external payment gateways (e.g. credit card), regulatory systems, and bank interfaces.** • **Enterprise Application Integration Services** • **Financial Management solution real-time, near real-time, batch integration with other business functions (e.g. CRM, Rights and Royalties Management, Marketing, Order Management, Product Management, Procurement and Vendor Management, Legal, HR)** • **Legacy systems integration during transition phase** • **Technology Standardization** • **Technology standards and best practices related to Financial Management solution** • **Data Standardization** • **Standard canonicals for key business entities (e.g. Customer Accounts, Payables, Receivable, Payments) that Financial Management solutions leverage** • **Application rationalization—Financial Management Solution** • **Consolidation of geo-specific and product specific functionalities and multiple versions of packaged solutions to support global Financial Management solution** • **Infrastructure Strategy** • **Strategy toward infrastructure capabilities such as hosting, cloud computing and virtualization which in turn would drive the Financial Management solution**

TABLE 5.138

Finance Candidate Business Scenario

Step	Description
1.	Royalty payment distribution is scheduled at pre-determined intervals to get the accrued royalty payments for the authors. Scheduler service is leveraged to start the royalty payment distribution
2.	Royalty calculation is performed using royalty payment calculation business function. a) Contract information is referred using information services
3.	Payment advice is sent to finance management—Account Payable business functions
4.	Payment advice is processed and finance account payable is updated
5.	Vendor is notified of the payment details through notification service and payment details are sent to Royalties management as well for authors to view through portal
6.	Vendor comes to the portal and views the payments distributed to him

5.3.48.3 Traceability (Table 5.139)

TABLE 5.139

Finance: Traceability

Principles	• **Prefer Use over Buy over Build** • **Drive for Reusable Solution Building Blocks** • **Avoid Current State Driving/Constraining Future State Design** • **Delineate Architectural Responsibility** • **Comply to Standards** • **Base Architecture on Service Orientation**
Business Capabilities	• Localized user experience • Financial processes supporting content/service bundles • Develop, refine, communicate and execute enterprise technology strategy and execution • Technology incubation and R&D capabilities • Cost-effective technology management • Enterprise service management

5.3.49 Product Management

In this section, Product Management functional area is elaborated with key influencing factors, candidate business scenario.

5.3.49.1 Influencing Factors

Based on the current state observations, business capabilities and architecture principles, the following include key influencing factors that may drive directly or indirectly Product Management solution (Table 5.140).

TABLE 5.140

Product Management Influencing Factors

Key Influencing Factors

• **Unified Portal for Product management**
  • Unified Portal solution for Product Lifecycle, Portfolio, Product Intelligence and Product performance management.
• **Multi-Channel Support Product Management User interfaces**
  • Product management user interface though channels such as web, mobile, email, tabletetc.
• **Adopting to Service Oriented Architecture**
  • SOA Strategy and Architecture design principles helps Product Management solution to be modular with separation of concerns
• **Foundations Services**
  • Availability of foundation Services to promote reusability and standards
• **Enterprise Integration Platform**
  • Integration platform required for solving P2P integration issues with Partner/Vendor Systems
• **Enterprise Application Integration Services**
  • Product Management solution real-time, near real-time, batch integration with other business functions (e.g. Content Management, Permission Systems, Order Management, Pricing and Discounts, Procurement and Vendor management, Financial Management, Marketing Management, CRM and Sales)
  • Legacy systems integration during transition phase
• **Technology Standardization**
  • Technology standards and best practices related to Product Management solution
• **Data Standardization**
  • Standard canonicals for key business entities (e.g. Product, Product item, Price, Product cost) that Product Management solutions leverage
• **Application rationalization—Product Management Solution**
  • Consolidation of geo-specific and product specific functionalities to support global Product Management solution
• **Infrastructure Strategy**
  • Strategy toward infrastructure capabilities such as hosting, cloud computing and virtualization which in turn would drive the Product Management solution

5.3.49.2 Product Management: Business Scenario

The following business scenario is selected to represents the sequence of interaction steps within architecture building blocks:

- Product Development

Scenarios validation helps to identify and/or validate any missing building blocks from presentation, process, business, and integration and foundation building blocks perspective, refine the responsibility of building blocks and alignment of fitness in the overall ecosystem.

- Product Development: Conceptualization (steps 1 to 2) (Table 5.141).

TABLE 5.141

Product Development Business Scenario: Conceptualization

1. **Marketing and Research teams determine the market need**
  a) Collects analysis data from product intelligence, sales, external retail analytics
2. **Develop Business Plan/Proposal (with financials)**
  a) Decision is made to develop proposal and Product proposal process is initiated
  b) Product is created in PDM and propagated to CMS

TABLE 5.142

Product Development Business Scenario: Proposal Development

---
3. **Set product Sales targets and devise marketing strategies and tactics**
   a) **Product price is determined through product pricing management and price and discounts function**
   b) **Sales target is sent to Finance**
4. **Solicit proposal feedback**
   c) **Collect the proposal feedback from internal and external through Marketing management**
5. **Revise till Proposal is Approved**
   d) **Iterate the proposal review till Product sales management approves it**

TABLE 5.143

Product Development Business Scenario: Contract

---
6. **Sign contracts**
   a) **Contract is signed**
7. **Finalize content plan**
   b) **Finalized content plan is setup in CMS**
8. **Setup Product**
   c) **Product information is updated in PDM**

- Product Development: Proposal Development (steps 3 to 5) (Table 5.142).
- Product Development: Contract (Steps 6 to 8) (Table 5.143).

5.3.49.3 Traceability (Table 5.144)

TABLE 5.144

Product Development: Traceability

Principles	• **Prefer Use over Buy over Build**
	• **Drive for Reusable Solution Building Blocks**
	• **Avoid Current State Driving/Constraining Future State Design**
	• **Delineate Architectural Responsibility**
	• **Comply to Standards**
	• **Base Architecture on Service Orientation**
Business Capabilities	• Single product development workflow
	• Localized user experience
	• Flexible, automated promotion and pricing
	• Workflow to manage pricing from price creation to quote to order to invoicing
	• Support for market/ geography research, opportunity identification and business case/ model development
	• Support for rapid prototyping, piloting and evaluation of new products and services
	• Product and program performance and lifecycle management
	• Develop, refine, communicate and execute enterprise technology strategy and execution
	• Technology incubation and R&D capabilities
	• Cost-effective technology management
	• Enterprise service management

5.3.50 BI & Reporting

The In this section, BI & Reporting functional area is elaborated with key influencing factors, candidate business scenarios. It also captures traceability of the functional area with pain points, principles and business capabilities.

TABLE 5.145

BI & Reporting Influencing Factors

Key Influencing factors

- **Unified Portal for BI and Reporting**
  - **Unified Portal solution for Cross functional reports and Dashboards.**
- **Multi-Channel Support BI and Reporting**
  - **Customer Analytical data captured from multiple channels such as Web, Mobile, Tablets, IVR, social networking**
- **Adopting to Service Oriented Architecture**
  - **SOA Strategy and Architecture design principles helps BI and Reporting Management solution to be modular with separation of concerns**
- **Foundations Services**
  - **Availability of Foundation Services to promote reusability and standards**
- **Enterprise Integration Platform**
  - **Integration platform required for solving P2P integration issues with External Analytical data Providers (e.g. Amazon)**
- **Enterprise Application Integration Services**
  - **BI and Reporting Management solution—real-time, near real-time, batch integration with other business functions (e.g. Product Management, CRM, Order Management, Financial Management, Portal, MDM platforms)**
  - **Legacy systems integration during transition phase**
- **Technology Standardization**
  - **Technology standards and best practices related to BI and Reporting Management solution**
- **Data Standardization**
  - **Standard canonicals for key business entities that BI and Reporting Management solutions leverage.**
- **Application rationalization—BI and Reporting Management Solution**
  - **Consolidation of geo-specific and product specific functionalities, multiple products (Web trends, Omniture, Google Analytics), multiple reporting solution, to enable global BI and Reporting solution.**
- **Infrastructure Strategy**
  - **Strategy toward infrastructure capabilities such as hosting, cloud computing and virtualization which in turn would drive the BI and Reporting Management solution**

5.3.50.1 Influencing Factors

The following are the representative key influencing factors (but not limited to) that may drive directly or indirectly Dynamic Content Management solution (Table 5.145).

5.3.50.2 BI and Reporting: Scenario

The following business scenario is selected to depict the sequence of interaction steps within architecture building blocks:

- Customer is online—Product Analytics is displayed
  - o People who bought this also bought these
  - o Top selling products by category
  - o Details of products customer browsed before

Scenarios validation helps to identify and/or validate any missing building blocks from presentation, process, business, and integration and foundation building blocks perspective, refine the responsibility of building blocks and alignment of fitness in the overall ecosystem.

TABLE 5.146

BI & Reporting Candidate Business Scenario

Customer orders via eCommerce portal—Data Acquisition

1. Customer logs into portal and browse various products
2. Customer chose a set of product and initiates ordering process
3. Ordering process leverages respective order management business services to fulfill the order
4. Completed customer order is stored in order data source

Customer order data is analyzed and prepared

5. Completed raw order data is stored into Analytics data store
6. Order data is analyzed by business analytics engine for various patterns/requirements then prepared and stored in Analytics data store

Customer behavior at portal is captured then analyzed and prepared

7. Customer's browsing activities are captured by Web Analytics engine and stored in Analytics data source
8. Customer activity data is analyzed by business analytics engine for various patterns/requirements then prepared and stored in Analytics data store

Prepared analytical data is displayed at eCommerce portal with respect to customer activity

9. Customer logs into portal and browse various products
10. Based on customer, product and activity portal requests Web Analytics service for pre-prepared analytical data from Analytics data source
11. Portal leverages Web 2.0 features (e.g. AJAX, RIA) and social networking (e.g. Facebook, blog) to get and render the value-added analytical data at Customer screen

---

Table 5.146 represents the sequence of interaction steps for **Customer eCommerce Experience** business scenario of BI & Reporting within architecture building blocks: Customer eCommerce Experience (Analytical Data).

5.3.50.3 Traceability Table 5.147

TABLE 5.147

BI & Reporting: Traceability

Principles	• **Prefer Use over Buy over Build** • **Drive for Reusable Solution Building Blocks** • **Avoid Current State Driving/Constraining Future State Design** • **Delineate Architectural Responsibility** • **Base Architecture on Service Orientation** • **Comply to Standards**
Business Capabilities	• Capture enterprise-wide view of customer including all of their interactions • Support for market/geography research, opportunity identification and business case/model development • Localized user experience • Content translated into appropriate local languages as demanded by market • Develop, refine, communicate and execute enterprise technology strategy and execution • Technology incubation and R&D capabilities • Cost-effective technology management • Enterprise service management

5.4 Conclusion

In this chapter, the Use Case 'Display Balance' has been modeled with Unified Modeling Language (UML) diagrams (Class Diagrams and Sequence Diagrams). UML is adequate for representing static relationships (Class Diagrams). However, UML is inadequate for representing dynamic properties (Sequence Diagrams). Moreover, UML notation is marked by semi-formality due to the absence of well-defined semantics. The Class and Sequence Diagrams are two separate artifacts in UML lacking integrity check. To prevail over these drawbacks, we put forward a formalized modeling framework in the next chapter toward an inclusive knowledge repository to cater to both static and dynamic features of a system.

Also, this chapter provided a discourse on Enterprise Architecture (EA)/Service-Oriented Architecture. The Architectural approach forms the basis of the book.

6

Knowledge Representation Using Predicate Calculus

6.1 Introduction

Merger & Acquisition (M&A) scenario requires consolidation of business processes of participating organizations, performing like independent business units (virtual consolidation), so that the operations of each participating entities are conserved. This is achieved using the methodology mentioned in the upcoming sections.

6.2 Process/Service Depiction with Predicate Calculus

The Service "showFunds" for "Banking organization" is a goal in AI [68]. The goal for Banking_Organization1 (Figure 6.1) is the expression: showFunds (Banking Organization1). This is represented by the implication:

```
{client (A) ∧ message (client (A), banking_organization (F), showFunds
(BankAccountNo)) ∧ message (banking_organization (F), system (G),
showFunds (BankAccountNo)) ∧ message (system (G),  bank_account(J),
getAccountNo ( )) → showFunds (banking_organization1)
```

The sub-goals are:

```
client (A), message (client (A), banking _organization (F), showFunds
(BankAccountNo)), message (banking_organization (F), system (G),
showFunds(BankAccountNo)), message (system (G), bank_account(J),
getAccountNo ( ))
```

The services (goal) for Bank2 (Figure 6.2) is the expression: showFunds (Banking Organization2), represented by:

```
{client (B) ∧ message (client (B), banking_organization (H), showFunds
(BankAccountNo)) ∧message (banking_organization (H), banking_
organization (H), showFunds(BankAccountNo)) ∧ message (banking_
organization (H), bank_account (K), getAccountNo ( )) → showFunds
(banking_organization2)
```

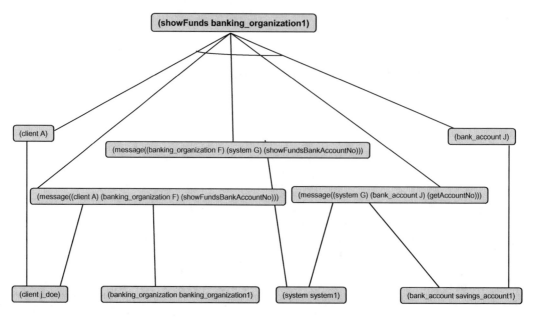

FIGURE 6.1
Solution Sub graph for Bank 1.

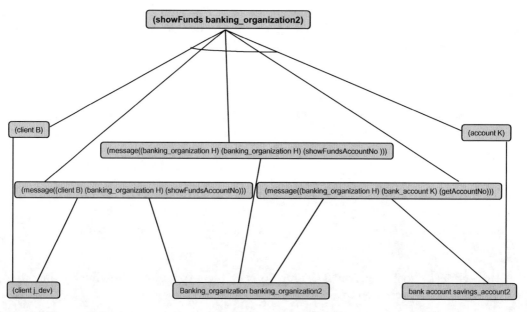

FIGURE 6.2
Solution Sub graph for Bank 2.

Services (goals) thus defined are WFF (Well Formed Formulae), with well-defined syntax & semantics and become part of the Knowledge Base.

Similarly, the services discussed in the discourse on EA/SOA can be realized through the Knowledge Based model.

6.3 Solution Graphs

The graphical illustration makes use of predicate calculus terminology in list syntax.

6.3.1 Solution Sub Graph for Banking_Organization1 (Figure 6.1)

The unifications which fulfill the sub goals are returned by the pattern_search algorithm, as furnished below. Security through authentication is intrinsic in the unification/substitution process:

```
{j_doe/A}, {banking_organization1/F}, {system1/G}, {savings_account1/J}
```

6.3.2 Solution Sub graph for Banking_Organization2

The Solution Sub graph for Banking_Organization2 has been furnished in Figure 6.2.

The unifications which fulfill the sub goals are returned by the pattern_search algorithm, as furnished below. Security through authentication is intrinsic in the unification/substitution process:

```
{j_dev/B}, {banking_organization2/H}, {savings_account2/K}
```

6.4 Process Composition

The Goal (Consolidated Service) is the expression for the new entity (say, mergedbank): showFunds (banking_organization_ mergedbank), represented by: showFunds (banking_ organization1) ∨ showFunds (banking_organization2) → showFunds (banking_organization_ mergedbank). Per Petri nets terminology, the foregoing represents OR-Split / Or-Join, applicable if the client is either a client of banking_organization1 OR banking_organization2, but not client of both.

For AND-Split/AND-Join:

```
showFunds (banking_organization1) ∧ showFunds (banking_organization2) →
showFunds (banking_organization_ mergedbank)
```

The consolidated service showFunds (banking_organization_ mergedbank) is combination/orchestration of services showFunds (banking_organization1) and showFunds (banking_organization2).

The above services (goals) are WFF (Well Formed Formulae) with appropriate syntax & semantics, consequently ensuring quality. The inferences (services/goals) turn into components of the Knowledge Base (KB). Various categories of services such as synchronous, asynchronous, manual, etc. can also be denoted by predicates. Predicates can also express Business Rules which may also be defined by means of Production Rule based Expert System (The Multi-use Service, mentioned subsequently).

6.5 The Knowledge Base

Representative set of Predicate Calculus expressions:

1. class (banking_organization)
2. banking_organization (banking_organization1)
3. banking_organization1 (showFunds ())
4. class (system)
5. system (private (int (Bank AccountNo)), (showFunds()))
6. multiplicity (banking_organization, system, one)
7. abstractclass (bank_account)
8. bank_account (protected (int (BankAccountNo)), protected (int (AccountBalance)), depositFund ( ), withdrawFund(),int(getAccountNo()))
9. abstractclass (checking_account)
10. subclass (bank_account, checking_account)
11. savings_account (protected (int(InterestRate)), creditInterest ( ))
12. checking_account (protected (int (checkNo, encashCheck())
13. subclass (bank_account, savings_account)
14. subclass (checking_account, individual_account)
15. subclass (checking_account, corporate_account)
16. corporate_account (addParty())
17. has (client, bank_account)
18. multiplicity (banking_organization, bank_account, many)
19. multiplicity (client, bank_account, many)
20. navigation (banking_organization, system, unidirectional)
21. navigation (banking_organization, bank_account, unidirectional)
22. class (client)
23. client (private (string (Name)), private (int (PhoneNo)), private (string (Address)))
24. navigation (bank_account, client, bi-directional)
25. system (system1)
26. banking_organization (banking_organization1)

27. banking_organization (banking_organization2)
28. client (j_doe)
29. j_doe(john_doe,9876543210,po_box_20_CD_Avenue_LA)
30. has (j_doe, savings_account1)
31. savings_account (savings_account1)
32. savings_account1 (1234,2500,5)
33. banking_organization2 (private(int(BankAccountNo)),showFunds())
34. equivalent(InterestRate,RateofInterest)
35. equivalent(CheckNumber, CheckNo)
36. client (j_dev)
37. savings_account (savings_account2)
38. has (j_dev, savings_account2)
39. savings_account2 (4321,5000,6)
40. j_dev(john_dev,1234567890,street_55_number_20_XY_Avenue_Beaverton)

Predicate Calculus is capable of representing comprehensively static structure features of UML including inheritance, composition, aggregation, etc.

Note:

- Predicates representing relationships between zero or more objects are expressed in lower case
- Variables start with upper case
- Constants are in lower case
- Functions start with lower case
- Knowledge Base can be distributed or centralized depending on the requirement scenario

6.6 Multi-use Service

The multi-use service is realized by a rule-based expert system, such as:

Rule A

```
If
Name matches with Name in Banking_Organization1 Knowledge Base, and
Address Information matches with Address Information in Banking_
Organization1 Knowledge Base
Then
Client is customer of Banking_Organization1
```

Rule B

```
If
Name matches with Name in Banking_Organization2 Knowledge Base, and
Address Information matches with Address Information in Banking_
Organization2 Knowledge Base
Then
Client is customer of Banking_Organization2
```

Rule C

```
If
Name matches with Name in Banking_Organization1& Banking_Organization2
Knowledge Bases, and
Address Information tallies with Address Information in Banking_
Organization1& Banking_Organization2 Knowledge Bases
Then
Client is customer of both Banking_Organization1&Banking_Organization2
```

Rule D

```
If
PhoneNo matches with PhoneNo in Banking_Organization1 Knowledge Base, and
Address matches with Address in Banking_Organization1 Knowledge Base
Then
Address Information matches with Address Information in Banking_
Organization1 Knowledge Base.
```

The problem is visually represented in Figure 6.3.

The goal in the system memory (Figure 6.4) is 'The Client is customer of both Banks'.

The rules (e.g.,Rule A, Rule B and Rule C) are in the system memory. If Rule A fires, this will mean'The Client is a customer of Banking_Organization1' and Rule A is placed in system memory (Figure 6.5). The system has selected an 'Or' branch in Figure 6.3.

For Rule A to trigger, the prerequisite is 'And' branches of the search graph, i.e. whether Name matches with Name in Banking_Organization1 Knowledge Base, and Address Information matches with Address Information in Banking_Organization1 Knowledge Base, is true. Then Rule D triggers, that is 'Address Information matches with Address Information in Banking_Organization1 Knowledge Base'.Thus, its premises are placed in memory (Figure 6.6).

If the system is unsuccessful to establish that the client is a customer of Banking_Organization1, then Rule 2 is tried after retracing to top level.

Following is the reasoning (the memory is as represented in Figure 6.6).

```
Is your Phone Number 9876543210?
Yes
Is your Address po_box_20_CD_Avenue_LA?
```

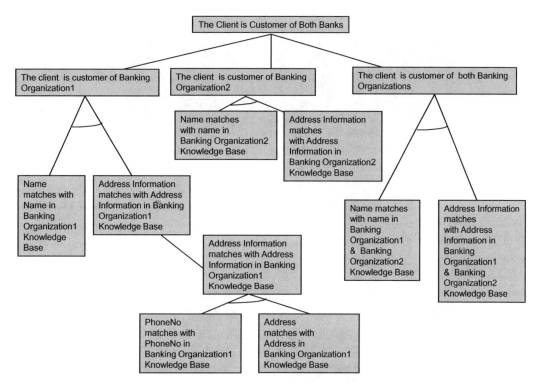

FIGURE 6.3
Visual Representation.

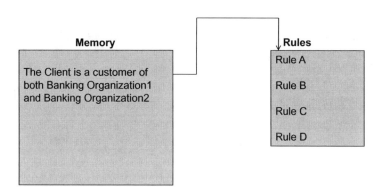

FIGURE 6.4
The Start of Transaction.

```
Yes
Is your Name john_doe?
Why
The system responds:
Address Information matches with Address Information in Banking_
Organization1 Knowledge Base,
Therefore, if
```

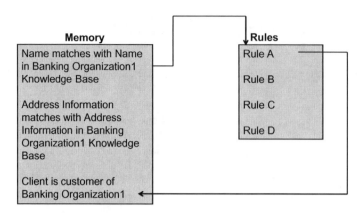

FIGURE 6.5
The System considering Rule A has Triggered.

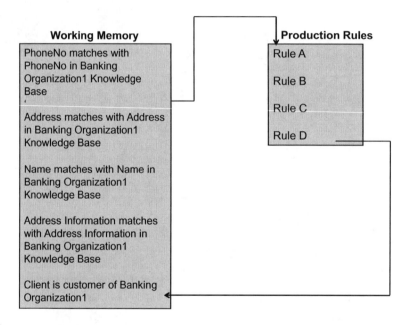

FIGURE 6.6
The System Considering Rule D has Triggered.

```
Name matches with Name in Banking_Organization1 Knowledge Base
You are a customer of Banking_Organization1.
```

Following the aforementioned transactions, the client's funds will be shown.
   The Client replied in the affirmative to the first two queries, and thus Rule D triggered.
   The client subsequently may query:
   How the Address Information matches with Banking_Organization1 Knowledge Base
   Response from the system will be as follows:

```
If: PhoneNo matches with PhoneNo in Banking_Organization1 Knowledge Base,
and
```

```
Address matches with Address in Banking_Organization1 Knowledge Base
Then
Address Information matches with Address Information in
Banking_Organization1
PhoneNo provided by Client
Address provided by Client
```

Thus, it is observed from the foregoing that authentication is achieved. The system could also be used for achieving authorization based on role / permission e.g.

Rule E

```
If
Role matches with Role in Banking_Organization1 Knowledge Base, and
Address Information matches with Address Information in Banking_
Organization1 Knowledge Base
Then
Client is authorized to useBanking_Organization1Knowledge Base
```

Further Examples of Business Rules

If the customer has ONLRC product
Then, Product ONLR0 can be ordered

If the customer has ONLRA product and not ONLRH product in his inventory
Then, Product ONLRs1 can be ordered

If the customer has both the products ONLRH and ONLRA in his inventory
Then, Product ONLR2 can be ordered

If the customer does not have both ONLRA and ONLRC products in inventory
Then, Product ONLRI can be ordered

If the customer is a new customer and if he does not have any KAI or KAV product in his inventory
Then, Product A01 can be ordered

If the customer is a new customer and if he does not have any KAI or KAV product in his inventory
Then, Product AAA can be ordered

If the customer is a new customer and if he does not have any KAI or KAV product in his inventory
Then, Product AAB can be ordered

If the customer has AAC product in his inventory
Then, Product AAC can be ordered

If the customer has AAC:001 product in his inventory
Then, Product AAC can be ordered

If the customer has AAC:003 product in his inventory
Then, Product AAC can be ordered

If the customer has AAC:B03 product in his inventory
Then, Product AAC can be ordered

If the customer is a new customer and if he does not have any KAI or KAV product in his inventory
Then, Product AC0 can be ordered

If the customer has KAI or KAV products in his inventory
Then, Product AC0 can be ordered

If the customer is a new customer and if he does not have any KAI or KAV product in his inventory
Then, Product AC1 can be ordered

If the customer is a new customer and if he does not have any KAI or KAV product in his inventory
Then, Product AC2 can be ordered

If the customer is a new customer and if he does not have any KAI or KAV product in his inventory
Then, Product AP2 can be ordered

If the customer is a new customer and if he does not have any KAI or KAV product in his inventory
Then, Product AP3 can be ordered

If the customer has AP3:012 product in his inventory
Then, Product AP3 can be ordered

If the customer has AP3:012 product in his inventory
Then, Product AP3 can be ordered

If the customer is a new customer and if he does not have any KAI or KAV product in his inventory
Then, Product AP6 can be ordered

If the customer is a new customer and if he does not have any KAI or KAV product in his inventory
Then, Product AP9 can be ordered

If the customer is a new customer and if he does not have any KAI or KAV product in his inventory
Then, Product APD can be ordered

If the customer has APM product in his inventory
Then, Product APM can be ordered

If the customer has APM product in his inventory
Then, Product AM1 can be ordered

If the customer is a new customer and if he does not have any KAI or KAV product in his inventory
Then, Product BF2 can be ordered

If the customer has TK_KAI OR BK_KAI product in his inventory
Then, Product BF6 can be ordered

If the customer is a new customer and if he does not have any KAI or KAV product in his inventory
Then, Product BF6 can be ordered

If the customer is a new customer and if he does not have any KAI or KAV product in his inventory
Then, Product BF7 can be ordered

If the customer has BFD product in his inventory
Then, Product BFD can be ordered

If the customer is a new customer and if he does not have any KAI or KAV product in his inventory
Then, Product GU2 can be ordered

If the customer is a new customer and if he does not have any KAI or KAV product in his inventory
Then, Product GW1 can be ordered

If the customer is a new customer and if he does not have any KAI or KAV product in his inventory
Then, Product GW2 can be ordered

If the customer is a new customer and if he does not have any KAI or KAV product in his inventory
Then, Product GW4 can be ordered

If the customer is a new customer and if he does not have any KAI or KAV product in his inventory
Then, Product GW5 can be ordered

If the customer is a new customer and if he does not have any KAI or KAV product in his inventory
Then, Product GW7 can be ordered

If the customer is a new customer and if he does not have any KAI or KAV product in his inventory
Then, Product GW8 can be ordered

If the customer is a new customer and if he does not have any KAI or KAV product in his inventory
Then, Product HB0 can be ordered

If the customer has KAI or KAV products in his inventory
Then, Product HB1 can be ordered

If the customer is a new customer and if he does not have any KAI or KAV product in his inventory
Then, Product HB2 can be ordered

If the customer has KAI or KAV products in his inventory
Then, Product HB3 can be ordered

If the customer is a new customer and if he does not have any KAI or KAV product in his inventory
Then, Product I01 can be ordered

If the customer is a new customer and if he does not have any KAI or KAV product in his inventory
Then, Product I02 can be ordered

If the customer has KAI or KAV products in his inventory
Then, Product IO3 can be ordered

If the customer has KAI or KAV products in his inventory
Then, Product IO4 can be ordered

If the customer is a new customer and if he does not have any KAI or KAV product in his inventory
Then, Product I05 can be ordered

If the customer has KAI or KAV products in his inventory
Then, Product Io6 can be ordered

If the customer is a new customer and if he does not have any KAI or KAV product in his inventory
AND the service category AP is not available at this service address
Then, Product IPO can be ordered

If the customer is a new customer and if he does not have any KAI or KAV product in his inventory
AND the service category AP is not available at this service address
Then, Product IPS can be ordered

If the customer has KAI or KAV products in his inventory
Then, Product OBI can be ordered

If the customer address is classified as NE4M28 address
AND If the customer is a new customer and if he does not have any KAI or KAV product in his inventory
Then, Product OI1 can be ordered

If the customer is a new customer and if he does not have any KAI or KAV product in his inventory
Then, Product OI2 can be ordered

If the customer has TK_KAI product in his inventory
Then, Product OI4 can be ordered

If the customer is a new customer and if he does not have any KAI or KAV product in his inventory
Then, Product PS0 can be ordered

If the customer is a new customer and if he does not have any KAI or KAV product in his inventory
Then, Product PS8 can be ordered

If the customer is a new customer and has KAV in his inventory
Then, Product RNRN can be ordered

If the customer is an existing customer and has KAV in his inventory
Then, Product RNRPC can be ordered

If the customer is an existing customer and has KAV in his inventory
Then, Product RNRPFN can be ordered

If the customer is an existing customer and has KAV in his inventory
Then, Product RNRPFY can be ordered

If the customer is a new customer and has KAV in his inventory
Then, Product RNRW1 can be ordered

If the customer is a new customer and has KAV in his inventory
Then, Product RNRWM can be ordered

If the customer is a new customer and has KAV in his inventory
Then, Product RNRWZ can be ordered

If the customer has KAI or KAV products in his inventory
Then, Product S99 can be ordered

If the customer is a new customer and if he does not have any KAI or KAV product in his inventory
Then, Product T11 can be ordered

If the customer has KAI or KAV products in his inventory
Then, Product T11BK can be ordered

If the customer is a new customer and if he does not have any KAI or KAV product in his inventory
Then, Product TA1 can be ordered

If the customer is a new customer and if he does not have any KAI or KAV product in his inventory
Then, Product TA5 can be ordered

If the customer has TAC product in his inventory
Then, Product TAC can be ordered

If the customer has TAC:B03 product in his inventory
Then, Product TAC can be ordered

If the customer has TAE product in his inventory
Then, Product TAE can be ordered

If the customer is a new customer and has KAV in his inventory
Then, Product TOEVL can be ordered

If the customer is a new customer and has KAV in his inventory
Then, Product TOEVN can be ordered

If the customer is a new customer and has KAV in his inventory
Then, Product TOEVS can be ordered

If the customer is a new customer and has KAV in his inventory
Then, Product TOSP can be ordered

If the customer has TOSPSZ product in his inventory
Then, Product TOSPSB can be ordered

If the customer has TOSPSB product in his inventory
Then, Product TOSPSZ can be ordered

If the customer is a new customer and has KAV in his inventory
Then, Product TOTBA can be ordered

If the customer is a new customer and has KAV in his inventory
Then, Product TOTBDV can be ordered

If the customer is a new customer and has KAV in his inventory
Then, Product TOTBEV can be ordered

If the customer is a new customer and has KAV in his inventory
Then, Product TOTBI can be ordered

If the customer is a new customer and has KAV in his inventory
Then, Product TOTBN can be ordered

If the customer is a new customer and has KAV in his inventory
Then, Product TOTBO can be ordered

If the customer is a new customer and has KAV and does not have KT_SOH product in his inventory
Then, Product TOTBVV can be ordered

If the customer is a new customer and has KAV in his inventory
Then, Product TOTBY can be ordered

If the customer is a new customer and has KAV in his inventory
Then, Product TOVDL can be ordered

If the customer is a new customer and has KAV in his inventory
Then, Product TOVDS can be ordered

If the customer is a new customer and if he does not have any KAI or KAV product in his inventory
Then, Product W01 can be ordered

If the customer is a new customer and if he does not have any KAI or KAV product in his inventory
Then, Product W02 can be ordered

If the customer is a new customer and if he does not have any KAI or KAV product in his inventory
Then, Product W09 can be ordered

If the customer is a new customer and if he does not have any KAI or KAV product in his inventory
Then, Product W13 can be ordered

If the customer is a new customer and if he does not have any KAI or KAV product in his inventory
Then, Product W14 can be ordered

If the customer has KAI or KAV products in his inventory
Then, Product W93 can be ordered

If the customer has KAI or KAV products in his inventory
Then, Product W95 can be ordered

If the customer is a new customer and if he does not have any KAI or KAV product in his inventory
Then, Product W96 can be ordered

If the customer has KAI or KAV products in his inventory
Then, Product W97 can be ordered

If the customer has KAI or KAV products in his inventory
Then, Product W98 can be ordered

If the customer is a new customer and if he does not have any KAI or KAV product in his inventory
Then, Product WA1 can be ordered

If the customer is a new customer and if he does not have any KAI or KAV product in his inventory
Then, Product WA2 can be ordered

If the customer is a new customer and if he does not have any KAI or KAV product in his inventory
Then, Product WA3 can be ordered

If the customer is a new customer and if he does not have any KAI or KAV product in his inventory
Then, Product WA4 can be ordered

If the customer is a new customer and if he does not have any KAI or KAV product in his inventory
Then, Product WA6 can be ordered

If the customer has KAI or KAV products in his inventory
Then, Product WB3 can be ordered

If the customer has KAI or KAV products in his inventory
Then, Product WB4 can be ordered

If the customer has KAI or KAV products in his inventory
Then, Product WB5 can be ordered

If the customer has XAA product in his inventory
Then, Product XAA can be ordered

If the customer has XAB product in his inventory
Then, Product XAB can be ordered

If the customer has XAC product in his inventory
Then, Product XAC can be ordered

If the customer has XAD product in his inventory
Then, Product XAD can be ordered

If the customer has XAE product in his inventory
Then, Product XAE can be ordered

[If the customer address is classified as NE3 OR NE4-VVO address
AND the customer is a NK_KAA customer]
OR
[If the customer address is classified as NE3 address
AND the customer is a BK_KAA customer]
Then, Product 346 can be ordered

If the customer address is classified as NE4-VVO address
AND the customer is a NK_KAA customer
Then, Product 44K can be ordered

If the customer address is classified as NE4-ZIB address
AND the customer is a NK_KAA customer
Then, Product 4BP can be ordered

If the customer address is classified as NE4-ZIB OR NE4-VVO address
AND the customer is a NK_KAA customer
Then, Product 4EP can be ordered

If the customer address is classified as NE4-VVO address
AND the customer is a NK_KAA customer
Then, Product 4KE can be ordered

If the customer address is classified as NE4-VVO address
AND the customer is a NK_KAA customer
Then, Product 4KP can be ordered

If the customer address is classified as NE4-VVO address
AND the customer is a NK_KAA customer
Then, Product 4ME can be ordered

If the customer address is classified as NE4-ZIB address
AND the customer is a NK_KAA customer
Then, Product 4MP can be ordered

If the customer address is classified as NE3 address
AND the customer is a NK_KAA customer
AND the service category KAD is available at this service address
Then, Product END can be ordered

If the customer address is classified as NE3 address where are a maximum of 6 ports are available in a
  building
AND the customer is a NK_KAA customer
AND both the service categories KAI and KAD are available at this service address
Then, Product EHS can be ordered

If the customer address is classified as NE3 address
AND the customer is a NK_KAA customer
AND the service category KAD is available at this service address
Then, Product EN2 can be ordered

If the customer address is classified as NE3 address
AND the customer is a BK_KAA customer
Then, Product EN2 can be ordered

If the customer address is classified as NE3 address
AND the customer has one of these products (ENV,ENM,ENA,E24,E01,E02,EAJ,EAM,165,187,715,E25,ENW,E
  N1,EN2,EN3,EN3:X06,EN3:X12,EN4,EN7,EN7:A10,EN5,4KE,4ME,4ME:A12)in his inventory
AND the service category KAD is available at this service address
Then, Product EN3 can be ordered

If service category KAD is available at his service address
Then, Product EN3 can be ordered

If service category KAI is available at his service address
Then, Product EN3 can be ordered

If the customer address is classified as NE3 address
AND the customer has one of these products (ENV,ENM,ENA,E24,E01,E02,EAJ,EAM,165,187,715,E25,ENW,E
  N1,EN2,EN3,EN3:X06,EN3:X12,EN4,EN7,EN7:A10,EN5,4KE,4ME,4ME:A12)in his inventory
Then, Product EN4 can be ordered

If service category KAD is available at his service address
Then, Product EN6 can be ordered

If service category KAI is available at his service address
Then, Product EN6 can be ordered

If the customer address is classified as NE3 address
AND the customer is a NK_KAA customer
AND the service category KAD is available at this service address
Then, Product EN7 can be ordered

If service category KAD is available at his service address
Then, Product EN8 can be ordered

If service category KAI is available at his service address
Then, Product EN8 can be ordered

If the customer address is classified as NE3 address
AND the customer is a NK_KAA customer
AND the service category KAD is available at this service address
Then, Product EN9 can be ordered

If service category KAI is available at his service address
Then, Product EW1 can be ordered

If service category KAI is available at his service address
Then, Product EW2 can be ordered

If the customer address is classified as NE4-VVO address
AND the customer is a NK_KAA customer
AND the service category KAI is available at this service address
Then, Product EW2 can be ordered

[If the customer address is classified as NE3 OR NE4-VVO address
AND the customer has any of the products (ENV,ENM,ENA,E24,E01,E02,EAJ,EAM,165,187,715,E25,ENW,EN
 1,EN2,EN3,EN3:X06,EN3:X12,EN4,EN7,EN7:A10,EN5,4KE,4ME,4ME:A12,4ME,4ME:A12,EW2,EW2:A12,EW
 3#BK_KAA) in the inventory
AND the service category KAI is available at this service address]
OR
[If the customer address is classified as NE4-VVO address
AND the customer has any of the products (ENV,ENM,ENA,E24,E01,E02,EAJ,EAM,165,187,715,E25,ENW,EN
 1,EN2,EN3,EN3:X06,EN3:X12,EN4,EN7,EN7:A10,EN5,4KE,4ME,4ME:A12,4ME,4ME:A12,EW2,EW2:A12,EW
 3#BK_KAA) in the inventory
AND the service category KAI is available at this service address]
Then, Product EW3 can be ordered

If service category KAI is available at his service address
Then, Product EW3 can be ordered

If the customer address is classified as NE4-VVO address where are a maximum of 6 ports are available in a
 building
AND the customer is a NK_KAA customer
AND both the service categories KAI and KAD are available at this service address
Then, Product EWS can be ordered

If the customer address is classified as NE4-VVO address
AND the customer is a NK_KAA customer
AND both the service categories KAD and KAI are available at this service address
Then, Product EWS can be ordered

If the customer address is classified as NE3 OR NE4-VVO address
AND the customer is a NK_KAA customer
AND the service category KAI is available at this service address
Then, Product EX2 can be ordered

If the customer address is classified as NE3 OR NE4-VVO address
AND the customer has any of these products (ENV,ENM,ENA,E24,E01,E02,EAJ,EAM,165,187,715,E25,ENW,E
 N1,EN2,EN3,EN3:X06,EN3:X12,EN4,EN7,EN7:A10,EN5,4KE,4ME,4ME:A12) in his inventory
AND the service category KAI is available at this service address
Then, Product EX3 can be ordered

If the customer address is classified as NE3 OR NE4-VVO address
AND the customer is a NK_KAA customer
AND the service category KAI is not available at this service address
Then, Product EX4 can be ordered

If the customer address is classified as NE3 OR NE4-VVO address
AND the customer has any of these products (ENV,ENM,ENA,E24,E01,E02,EAJ,EAM,165,187,715,E25,ENW,E
  N1,EN2,EN3,EN3:X06,EN3:X12,EN4,EN7,EN7:A10,EN5,4KE,4ME,4ME:A12) in his inventory
AND the service category KAI is not available at this service address
Then, Product EX5 can be ordered

If the customer address is classified as NE4-VVO address
AND the customer is a NK_KAA customer
AND the service category KAD is available at this service address
Then, Product EX6 can be ordered

If the customer address is classified as NE3 address
AND the customer is a NK_KAA customer
AND the service category KAI is available at this service address
Then, Product EXY can be ordered

If service category KAD is available at his service address
Then, Product FN2 can be ordered

If the customer address is classified as NE3 address
AND the customer is a NK_KAA customer
AND the service category KAD is available at this service address
Then, Product L3A can be ordered

If the customer address is classified as NE4-VVO address
AND the customer is a NK_KAA customer
AND both the service categories KAI and KAD are available at this service address
Then, Product L4A can be ordered

If the customer address is classified as NE4-VVO address
AND the customer is a NK_KAA customer
AND the service categories KAD is available and KAI is not available at this service address
Then, Product L4N can be ordered

If the customer address is classified as NE3 address
AND the customer is a NK_KAA customer
AND the service category KAD is available at this service address
Then, Product M3A can be ordered

If the customer address is classified as NE4-VVO address
AND the customer is a NK_KAA customer
AND both the service categories KAI and KAD are available at this service address
Then, Product M4A can be ordered

If the customer address is classified as NE4-VVO address
AND the customer is a NK_KAA customer
AND the service categories KAD is available and KAI is not available at this service address
Then, Product M4N can be ordered

If the customer address is classified as NE4-VVO address
AND the customer is a NK_KAA customer
AND both the service categories KAI and KAD are available at this service address
Then, Product S4A can be ordered

If the customer address is classified as NE4-VVO address
AND the customer is a NK_KAA customer
AND the service categories KAD is available and KAI is not available at this service address
Then, Product S4N can be ordered

[If the customer address is classified as NE3 OR NE4-VVO address
AND the customer is a NK_KAA customer
AND the service category KAD is available at this service address]
OR
[If the customer address is classified as NE3address
AND the customer is a BK_KAA customer
AND the service category KAD is available at this service address]
Then, Product 499 can be ordered

If the customer address is classified as NE4-VVO address
AND the customer is a NK_KAA customer
AND the service category KAD is available at this service address
Then, Product VP0 can be ordered

If the customer address is classified as NE3 address
AND the customer is a NK_KAA customer
AND the service category KAD is available at this service address
Then, Product VP1 can be ordered

If the customer address is classified as NE3 address
AND the customer is a NK_KAA customer
AND the service category KAD is available at this service address
Then, Product VP2 can be ordered

If the customer does not have RC product in his inventory
Then, Product D24 can be ordered

If the customer has SC product in his inventory
Then, Product D3X can be ordered

If the customer has SC product in his inventory
Then, Product D6X can be ordered

If the customer does not have RC product in his inventory
Then, Product DA2 can be ordered

If the customer does not have RC product in his inventory
Then, Product DA4 can be ordered

If the customer does not have RC product in his inventory
Then, Product DEL can be ordered

If service category KAI is available at his service address
Then, Product DFH can be ordered

If the customer does not have RC product in his inventory
Then, Product DHL can be ordered

If the customer does not have SC product in his inventory
Then, Product DI0 can be ordered

If the customer does not have SC product in his inventory
Then, Product DI1 can be ordered

If the customer does not have SC product in his inventory
Then, Product DI2 can be ordered

If the customer does not have SC product in his inventory
Then, Product DI9 can be ordered

If the customer does not have SC product in his inventory
Then, Product DN6 can be ordered

If the customer does not have SC product in his inventory
Then, Product DN8 can be ordered

If the customer does not have SC product in his inventory
Then, Product DN9 can be ordered

If the customer has none of the products(D1H,D24,D24:P09,D24:P11,D2H,D2U,D3H,D4H,D5H,D6H,D6H:A02
,D6H:A03,D7H,D7H:A02,DA1,DA1:A01,DA1:A02,DA2,DA2:A02,DA3,DA3:A02,DA8,DA8:A02,DA9,DAH,D
AH:P09,DAR,DBH,DBH:A03,DGG,DH1,DH1:P06,DH2,DH3,DH3:AB5,DH3:P09,DH3:P10,DH3:P11,DH4,DH
6,DH6:P09,DH6:P10,DH6:P11,DH7,DH8,DHA,DHG,DHL,DHL:P06,DHL:P09,DHL:P11,DHP,DHP:P10,DHR,
DHS,DHS:P09,DHT,DHT:P09,DHV:P09,DHW,DHZ,DKH,DKH:P09,DKH:P10,DKH:P11,DMA,DP1,DP1:A02,
DP1:A09,DP1:A12,DP1:TUB,DP2,DP3,DP4,DP5,DP5:A03,DP6,DP7,DP7:AX3,DP7:AX6,DP8,DP9,DP9:A02,D
PL,DPM,DU1,DU3,DU4,DU5,DUX,DUY,DWA,DWB,MON) in his inventory
Then, Product DP4 can be ordered

If the customer has any one of the products(D1H,D24,D24:P09,D24:P11,D2H,D2U,D3H,D4H,D5H,D6H,D6H:
A02,D6H:A03,D7H,D7H:A02,DA1,DA1:A01,DA1:A02,DA2,DA2:A02,DA3,DA3:A02,DA8,DA8:A02,DA9,DA
H,DAH:P09,DAR,DBH,DBH:A03,DGG,DH1,DH1:P06,DH2,DH3,DH3:AB5,DH3:P09,DH3:P10,DH3:P11,DH
4,DH6,DH6:P09,DH6:P10,DH6:P11,DH7,DH8,DHA,DHG,DHL,DHL:P06,DHL:P09,DHL:P11,DHP,DHP:P10,
DHR,DHS,DHS:P09,DHT,DHT:P09,DHV:P09,DHW,DHZ,DKH,DKH:P09,DKH:P10,DKH:P11,DMA,DU1,DU
3,DU4,DU5,DUX,DUY,DWA,DWB,MON) in his inventory
Then, Product DP5 can be ordered

If the customer has any one of the products(DP1,DP1:A02,DP1:A09,DP1:A12,DP1:TUB,DP2,DP3,DP4,DP5,DP
5:A03,DP6,DP7,DP7:AX3,DP7:AX6,DP8,DP9,DP9:A02,DPM) in his inventory
Then, Product DP6 can be ordered

If the customer address is classified as NE3 address
AND the customer is a NK customer
AND the service category KAI is available at this service address
Then, Product DP7 can be ordered

If the customer has any one of the products(D1H,D24,D24:P09,D24:P11,D2H,D2U,D3H,D4H,D5H,D6H,D6H:
A02,D6H:A03,D7H,D7H:A02,DA1,DA1:A01,DA1:A02,DA2,DA2:A02,DA3,DA3:A02,DA8,DA8:A02,DA9,DA
H,DAH:P09,DAR,DBH,DBH:A03,DGG,DH1,DH1:P06,DH2,DH3,DH3:AB5,DH3:P09,DH3:P10,DH3:P11,DH
4,DH6,DH6:P09,DH6:P10,DH6:P11,DH7,DH8,DHA,DHG,DHL,DHL:P06,DHL:P09,DHL:P11,DHP,DHP:P10,
DHR,DHS,DHS:P09,DHT,DHT:P09,DHV:P09,DHW,DHZ,DKH,DKH:P09,DKH:P10,DKH:P11,DMA,DU1,DU
3,DU4,DU5,DUX,DUY,DWA,DWB,MON) in his inventory
Then, Product DP9 can be ordered

If the customer has any one of the products(D6H:A02,DA1,DA1:A01,DA1:A02,DA2,DA2:A02,DA3,DA3:A02,
DA8,DA8:A02,DA9) in his inventory
Then, Product DP9 can be ordered

If the customer has none of the products(D1H,D24,D24:P09,D24:P11,D2H,D2U,D3H,D4H,D5H,D6H,D6H:A02
,D6H:A03,D7H,D7H:A02,DA1,DA1:A01,DA1:A02,DA2,DA2:A02,DA3,DA3:A02,DA8,DA8:A02,DA9,DAH,D
AH:P09,DAR,DBH,DBH:A03,DGG,DH1,DH1:P06,DH2,DH3,DH3:AB5,DH3:P09,DH3:P10,DH3:P11,DH4,DH
6,DH6:P09,DH6:P10,DH6:P11,DH7,DH8,DHA,DHG,DHL,DHL:P06,DHL:P09,DHL:P11,DHP,DHP:P10,DHR,
DHS,DHS:P09,DHT,DHT:P09,DHV:P09,DHW,DHZ,DKH,DKH:P09,DKH:P10,DKH:P11,DMA,DP1,DP1:A02,
DP1:A09,DP1:A12,DP1:TUB,DP2,DP3,DP4,DP5,DP5:A03,DP6,DP7,DP7:AX3,DP7:AX6,DP8,DP9,DP9:A02,D
PL,DPM,DU1,DU3,DU4,DU5,DUX,DUY,DWA,DWB,MON) in his inventory
Then, Product DPC can be ordered

If the customer has any of the products(D1H,D24,D24:P09,D24:P11,D2H,D2U,D3H,D4H,D5H,D6H,D6H:A02,
D6H:A03,D7H,D7H:A02,DA1,DA1:A01,DA1:A02,DA2,DA2:A02,DA3,DA3:A02,DA8,DA8:A02,DA9,DAH,D
AH:P09,DAR,DBH,DBH:A03,DGG,DH1,DH1:P06,DH2,DH3,DH3:AB5,DH3:P09,DH3:P10,DH3:P11,DH4,DH
6,DH6:P09,DH6:P10,DH6:P11,DH7,DH8,DHA,DHG,DHL,DHL:P06,DHL:P09,DHL:P11,DHP,DHP:P10,DHR,
DHS,DHS:P09,DHT,DHT:P09,DHV:P09,DHW,DHZ,DKH,DKH:P09,DKH:P10,DKH:P11,DMA,DU1,DU3,DU
4,DU5,DUX,DUY,DWA,DWB,MON) in his inventory
Then, Product DPD can be ordered

If the customer does not have SC product in his inventory
Then, Product DSC can be ordered

If the customer has any of the products(DB1,DB2,DB3,DB4) in his inventory
Then, Product DU1 can be ordered

If the customer has DB1 product in his inventory
Then, Product DU3 can be ordered

If the customer has SC product in his inventory
Then, Product DX1 can be ordered

If the customer has SC product in his inventory
Then, Product DX2 can be ordered

If the customer has SC product in his inventory
Then, Product DX3 can be ordered

If the customer has SC product in his inventory
Then, Product DX4 can be ordered

If the customer has SC product in his inventory
Then, Product DX6 can be ordered

If the customer has DXX product in his inventory
Then, Product DXN can be ordered

If the customer has DIRECTHSP product in his inventory
Then, Product HSD can be ordered

If the customer is a new customer and has KAD in his inventory
Then, Product ID0 can be ordered

If the customer is a new customer and has KAD in his inventory
Then, Product ID1 can be ordered

If the customer is a new customer and has KAD in his inventory
Then, Product ID2 can be ordered

If the customer has SCS product in his inventory
Then, Product SCSWLM can be ordered

6.7 Architecture

The architecture illustration for our proposed AI Based Architecture is provided below (Figure 6.7).

The architecture comprises of horizontal tiers, comprised as follows:

- Knowledge Base: predicate calculus expressions
- Unification/Substitution: unifications that satisfies sub goals returned by the pattern_search algorithm
- Process/Services Realization:
  - o Sub-goals: e.g. "showFunds (BankAccountNo)"
  - o Goals: implications for each individual bank (Service "showFunds")
  - o Business scenario: consolidated services, e.g. showFunds (banking_organization_mergedbank)
- Vertical Tier:
  - o Business rule engine: Rule based expert system tier (applicable to sub-goal, goal and process/service composition tiers)

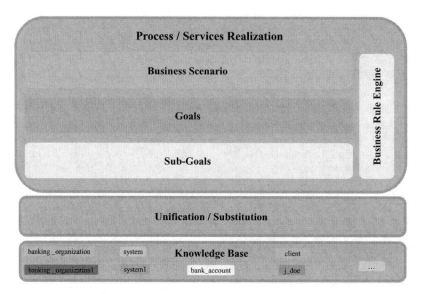

FIGURE 6.7
Proposed Architecture.

6.8 Conclusion

This chapter considers consolidation of business processes (represented by UML Diagrams) by means of AI (knowledge-based) approach, providing full-fledged representation of static and dynamic behavior of a system, applicable to financial and other domains.

7

Petri Net Modeling of Business Processes

7.1 Introduction

Dynamic behavior of a system is well represented by Petri net. However, Petri nets, though being formalized, are not useful for modeling of static relations, since they are not designed for that purpose.

7.2 Petri Net Framework/Architecture

The use case 'show funds' for Banking Organization1 is represented as composition of a couple of Petri nets, based on sender-receiver paradigm, wherein objects(e.g., Client, Banking_ Organization, System and Bank_ Account)are modeled as Places, messages being modeled as Transitions.

In Figure 7.1 the token is in the 'Client' place, thereby triggering the transition 'show-Funds', removing the token from the Client place and placing a token in the 'Banking_ Organization' place; now the transition 'showFunds' is enabled, removing the token from the 'Banking_ Organization' place. Thus, a token is placed in the 'System' place, enabling the transition 'getAccountNo', placing a token in the Banking_Account place.

In Figure 7.2 the places are swapped, the producer is the consumer/the sender is the receiver. After the token is placed in the Bank_Account place (Figure 7.2) a transition is triggered and the token is removed and this triggers the transition 'returnAccountNo', thus placing the token in the 'System' place, enabling the transition 'returnFunds', placing the token in the 'Banking_Organization' place, triggering a transition and putting a token in the 'Client' place.

The combined Petri net for Banking Organization1 is represented in Figure 7.3.

Likewise, the use case show funds for Banking Organization2 is shown in Figure 7.6. Figures 7.4 and 7.5 show individual Petri nets for Banking Organization2.

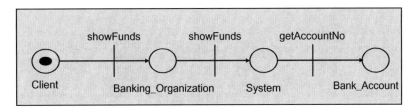

FIGURE 7.1
Petri net Model 1 (P11): Banking Organization1.

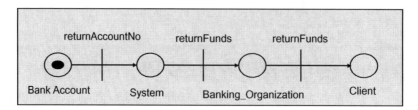

FIGURE 7.2
Petri net Model 2 (P12): Banking Organization1.

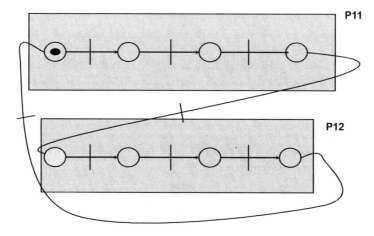

FIGURE 7.3
Combined Petri net Model for Banking Organization1 (P1).

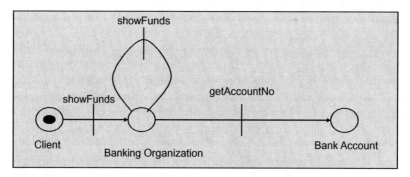

FIGURE 7.4
Petri net Model 1(P21): Banking Organization2.

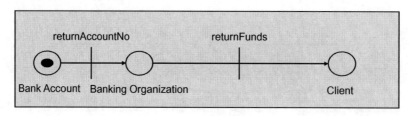

FIGURE 7.5
Petri net Model 1(P22): Banking Organization2.

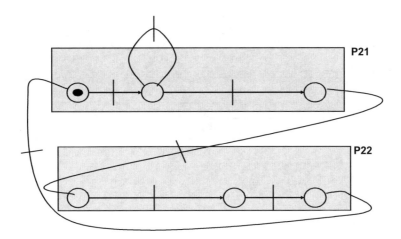

FIGURE 7.6
Combined Petri net Model for Banking Organization2 (P2).

7.3 Post-Consolidation Scenario

The possibilities are:

1. The client is an existing customer of Banking Organization1
2. The client is an existing customer of Banking Organization2
3. The client is an existing customer of both Banking Organizations

For possibilities 1 and 2, the Petri net of Banking Organization1, or that of Banking Organization2, is accessed based on Mutual Exclusion (Figure 7.7).

For possibility 3, the Petri nets of Banking Organization1 and Banking Organization 2 are accessed sequentially with Banking Organization1 process first, followed by Banking Organization 2 process, or vice-versa, ensuring prevention of any deadlock condition (Figure 7.8), and ensuring seamless conflict resolution service.

7.4 Petri Net Representation of Predicate Calculus Knowledge Base

We observe from the foregoing that Petri nets depict dynamic behavior of systems adequately. In this section we make an attempt toward representing the predicate calculus knowledge base of Chapter 6 by means of Petri nets.

Let us consider a few examples. The first predicate calculus expression in the knowledge base is class (banking_organization). This expression conveys that banking_organization is a class. The Petri net representation of the same is depicted in Figure 7.9a, where 'class' and 'banking_organization' are represented by places and 'is a' is represented by a transition. Similarly, Figures 7.9b and 7.9c shows that banking_organization1 is a banking_organization (the predicate calculus expression banking_organization(banking_organization1)).

Likewise, Petri nets can represent all the predicate calculus expressions in the knowledge base, which have been shown in Figures 7.10a to 7.21c.

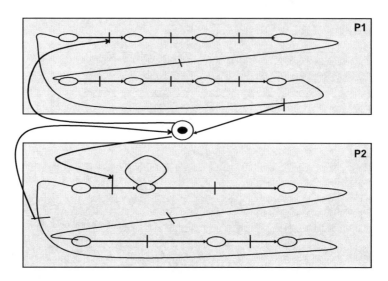

FIGURE 7.7
Post-Consolidation Scenario: Mutual Exclusion.

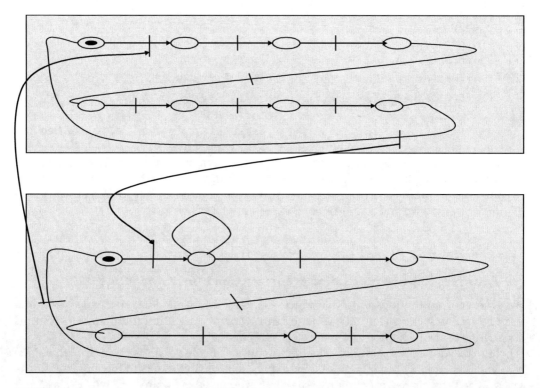

FIGURE 7.8
Post-Consolidation Scenario: Sequential Process.

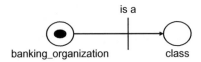

FIGURE 7.9a
Petri net Representation of Predicate Calculus Knowledge Base: class (banking_organization).

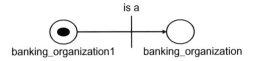

FIGURE 7.9b
Petri net Representation of Predicate Calculus Knowledge Base: banking_organization (banking_organization1).

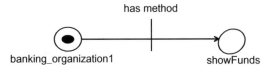

FIGURE 7.9c
banking_organization1 (showFunds()).

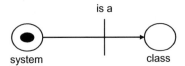

FIGURE 7.10a
Petri net Representation of Predicate Calculus Knowledge Base: class (system).

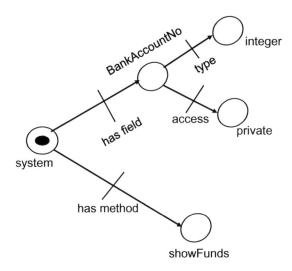

FIGURE 7.10b
Petri net Representation of Predicate Calculus Knowledge Base: system (private (int (BankAccountNo)), (showFunds())).

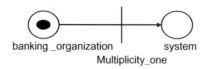

FIGURE 7.10c
Petri net Representation of Predicate Calculus Knowledge Base: multiplicity (banking_organization, system, one).

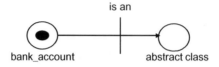

FIGURE 7.10d
Petri net Representation of Predicate Calculus Knowledge Base: abstractclass (bank_account).

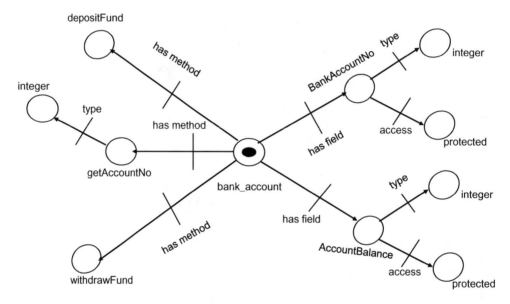

FIGURE 7.11
Petri net Representation of Predicate Calculus Knowledge Base: bank_account (protected (int (BankAccountNo)), protected (int (Balance)), deposit ( ), withdraw(), int(getAccountNo()))).

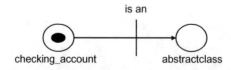

FIGURE 7.12a
Petri net Representation of Predicate Calculus Knowledge Base: abstractclass (checking_account).

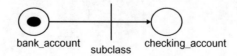

FIGURE 7.12b
Petri net Representation of Predicate Calculus Knowledge Base: subclass (bank_account,checking_account).

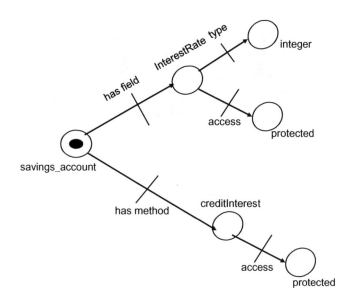

FIGURE 7.12c
Petri net Representation of Predicate Calculus Knowledge Base: savings_account (protected (int(InterestRate)), creditInterest ( )).

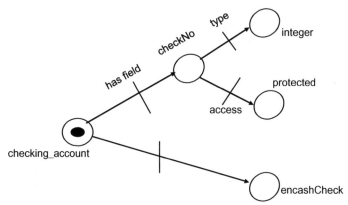

FIGURE 7.13a
Petri net Representation of Predicate Calculus Knowledge Base: checking_account (protected (int (checkNo), encashCheck()).

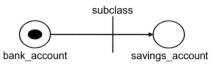

FIGURE 7.13b
Petri net Representation of Predicate Calculus Knowledge Base: subclass (bank_account, savings_account).

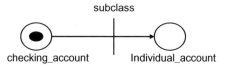

FIGURE 7.13c
Petri net Representation of Predicate Calculus Knowledge Base: subclass (checking_account,individual_account).

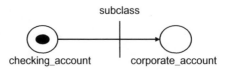

FIGURE 7.14a
Petri net Representation of Predicate Calculus Knowledge Base: subclass (checking_account,corporate_account).

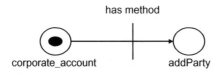

FIGURE 7.14b
Petri net Representation of Predicate Calculus Knowledge Base: corporate_account (addParty()).

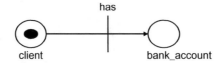

FIGURE 7.14c
Petri net Representation of Predicate Calculus Knowledge Base: has (client,bank_account).

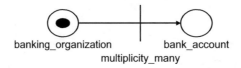

FIGURE 7.14d
Petri net Representation of Predicate Calculus Knowledge Base: multiplicity (banking_organization,bank_account, many).

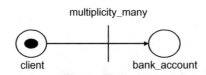

FIGURE 7.15a
Petri net Representation of Predicate Calculus Knowledge Base: multiplicity (client, bank_account, many).

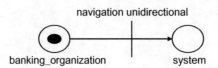

FIGURE 7.15b
Petri net Representation of Predicate Calculus Knowledge Base: navigation (banking_organization, system, unidirectional).

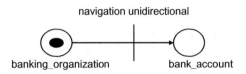

FIGURE 7.15c
Petri net Representation of Predicate Calculus Knowledge Base: navigation (banking_organization, bank_account, unidirectional).

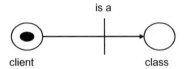

FIGURE 7.15d
Petri net Representation of Predicate Calculus Knowledge Base: class (client).

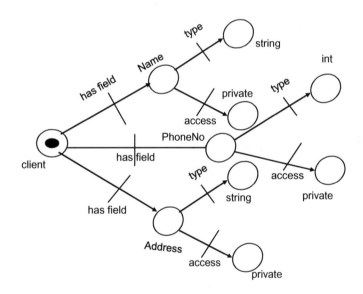

FIGURE 7.16a
Petri net Representation of Predicate Calculus Knowledge Base: client (private (string (Name)), private (int (PhoneNo)), private (string (Address))).

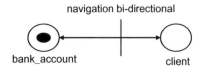

FIGURE 7.16b
Petri net Representation of Predicate Calculus Knowledge Base: navigation (bank_account, client, bi-directional).

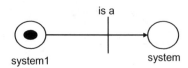

FIGURE 7.16c
Petri net Representation of Predicate Calculus Knowledge Base: system (system1).

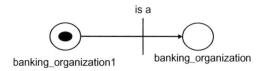

FIGURE 7.17a
Petri net Representation of Predicate Calculus Knowledge Base: banking_organization (banking_organization1).

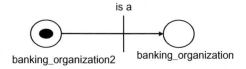

FIGURE 7.17b
Petri net Representation of Predicate Calculus Knowledge Base: banking_organization (banking_organization2).

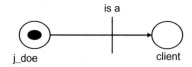

FIGURE 7.17c
Petri net Representation of Predicate Calculus Knowledge Base: client (j_doe).

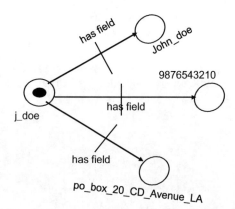

FIGURE 7.17d
Petri net Representation of Predicate Calculus Knowledge Base:j_doe (john_doe, 9876543210,po_box_20_CD_ Avenue_LA).

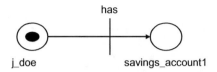

FIGURE 7.18a
Petri net Representation of Predicate Calculus Knowledge Base: has (j_doe, savings_account1).

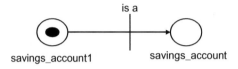

FIGURE 7.18b
Petri net Representation of Predicate Calculus Knowledge Base: savings_account (savings_account1).

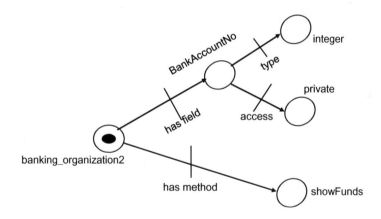

FIGURE 7.18c
Petri net Representation of Predicate Calculus Knowledge Base: banking_organization2 (private(int(Bank AccountNo)), showFunds()).

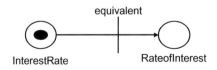

FIGURE 7.18d
Petri net Representation of Predicate Calculus Knowledge Base: equivalent (Interest Rate, Rate of Interest).

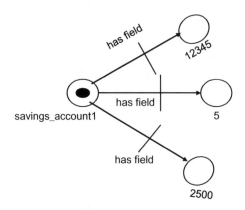

FIGURE 7.19a
Petri net Representation of Predicate Calculus Knowledge Base: savings_account1 (12345, 2500,5).

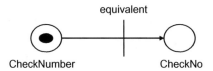

FIGURE 7.19b
Petri net Representation of Predicate Calculus Knowledge Base: equivalent (CheckNumber, CheckNo).

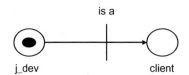

FIGURE 7.20a
Petri net Representation of Predicate Calculus Knowledge Base: client (j_dev).

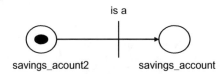

FIGURE 7.20b
Petri net Representation of Predicate Calculus Knowledge Base: savings_account (savings_account2).

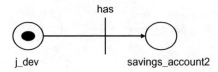

FIGURE 7.21a
Petri net Representation of Predicate Calculus Knowledge Base: has (j_dev, savings_account2).

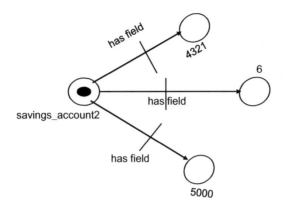

FIGURE 7.21b
Petri net Representation of Predicate Calculus Knowledge Base: savings_account2 (4321,5000,6).

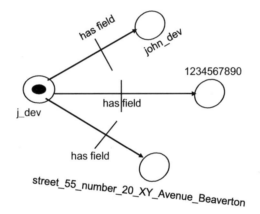

FIGURE 7.21c
Petri net Representation of Predicate Calculus Knowledge Base: j_dev (john_dev, 1234567890, street_55_number_
20_XY_Avenue_Beaverton).

7.5 Conclusion

From the aforementioned it is seen that that dynamic behavior of a system (e.g., business processes) is adequately represented by Petri nets, which depicts through visual representation when a process is triggered (through tokens and places).

Static structure knowledge can also be represented with Petri nets, as can be seen from this chapter, though the representation is relatively complex.

The knowledge-based architecture provides a comprehensive knowledge repository for static relationships and dynamic behavior including search & inferencing features, unavailable in UML and Petri net-based approaches, in Chapter 8.

8

Conclusion

AI (Knowledge) based process representation is an alternative methodology to UML and Petri net-based approaches. UML and Petri net are modeling approaches with limitations, However, the AI (Knowledge) based approach leads to comprehensive architecture encompassing static and dynamic features of a system.

8.1 Introduction

8.2 Improvements Achieved with AI (Knowledge) Based Approach

8.2.1 Comprehensive Modeling

Complete modeling of static and dynamic behavior of organizations, especially in the context of process orchestration/composition. Dynamic behavior is manifested by visual means of solution graphs.

8.2.2 Inferencing

The AI (Knowledge) based architecture implements goals WFF (Well Formed Formulae) which are service-oriented manifestation of processes, possessing proper syntax and semantics, which makes certain QoS (Quality of Services).

8.2.3 Service Discovery

Service discovery is through pattern search and substitution/unification.

8.2.4 Routing and Transformation

Messages are maintained in the Knowledge Base. Routing and data transformation are also defined as predicates in the Knowledge Base, or alternatively as part of the Expert system. The trade-off between the KB and the Expert system would be based on requirement analysis and QoS—Quality of Service factors (e.g. response time).

8.2.5 Flexibility

The KB or the Multi-use Service encompass Business Rules, Routing Logic and Transformation Logic.

Predicates can denote services in the Knowledge Base, such as manual, synchronous, asynchronous, etc. Rules may be defined in the Business Rule Engine (Multi-use service).

Business Rules such as OR-Split/OR-Join, or AND-Split/AND-Join will be taken care of by a Production Rule Based Expert System, which will also facilitate authorization of the user / customer.

8.2.6 Knowledge Base Based on Patterns

Relevant patterns such as Integration Patterns, Business Patterns, and Workflow Patterns can be modeled as predicate calculus expressions and retained in the Knowledge Base, which can be searched and retrieved by the Pattern Search and Unification/Substitution. This is a key strong point of the AI (Knowledge) based architecture.

8.2.7 BI

BI (Business Intelligence) is realized by knowledge discovery through inferences.

8.2.8 Security

Authentication is manifested through the unification/substitution process (discussed in Section 6.2 and 6.3). Role based authorization is realized by means of Multi-use Service (discussed in Section 6.6).

8.2.9 Quality

The AI (Knowledge) based architecture makes use of syntactically and semantically correct Well Formed Formulae (WFF) thereby ensuring quality of orchestrated / composed services.

8.2.10 Extensibility

The Multi-use Service described in the book is greatly configurable. Existing rules can be customized depending on shifting business scenarios. If necessary, rules can be deleted and new/additional rules added. Having the process logic practically fully rule driven will lead to exceedingly extensible and flexible, and hence, agile systems.

The discussed architecture is extensible depending on organizational need. Such as, if another Banking Organization is merged, the Knowledge Base would be able to encompass that by using suitable predicate calculus expressions. Thus, the AI based architecture is very much extensible.

8.2.11 Reusability

The services (Goals & Sub-goals) turn into constituents of the Knowledge Base and can be reused. Moreover, the Inferences derived from the Business Rules Engine can be integrated into the Knowledge Base, and reused.

8.2.12 Governance

This is achieved using the Rule driven Expert System. The system is very much configurable, and therefore the Policies for Governance can be amended in accordance with the dynamic business requirements.

8.3 New Perspectives and Contributions of the Book

- A new AI/Knowledge based process modeling framework as an alternative to established UML & Petri Net based modeling approaches. The utility of the AI/Knowledge Based approach in the architectural domain of Service-Oriented Architecture (SOA) has been explored.
- Comprehensive modeling of static and dynamic properties of a system/organization.
- A framework to facilitate Mergers & Acquisitions (M&As).
- The Fuzzy Mathematical Approach leads to unearthing of concealed knowledge, in real world terminology, enables the corporate decision maker to handle financial resources in the best possible way, and assess the feasibility of M&As.

8.4 Modeling Approaches: Comparison

UML	Petri Nets	Knowledge Base
Complete representation of static structure associations in a system/organization	Complex representation of static structure relationships	Predicate calculus knowledge base represents static structure relationships comprehensively
Restricted visual representation of dynamic behavior of a system	Dynamic behavior comprehensively represented, Business Process/Workflow modeling manifested by means of established & extended patterns	Visual dynamic behavior representation of a system through goal representation. AND/OR Rules in Knowledge Base represent basic Patterns & additional patterns represented as Inferences
Semiformal	Based on Semantic Network	Predicate Calculus based architecture (Syntactically & Semantically comprehensive)
No provision for rule engine	No provision for rule engine	Rule Engine based on expert system
Search provisions non-existent	Search provisions non-existent	Search provisions

- Modeling Approaches: Comparison:
  - o Static feature modeling
    - ■ AI architecture: higher simplicity

- Unified Modeling Language (UML): intermediate simplicity
- Petri Nets: lower simplicity

o Dynamic feature modeling

- Petri Nets: higher simplicity
- AI architecture: intermediate simplicity
- Unified Modeling Language (UML): lower simplicity

8.5 Scenarios Where the Framework Can Be Applied

- **Scenario 1**
  Objectives: To achieve process efficiency, loose coupling between systems and agility at Enterprise level
  Problem statement:

  - The organization's application portfolio has evolved over a period of time resulting in lack of standardized reference architecture
  - Redundant applications and higher total cost of ownership
  - Legacy Apps used for key business processes
  - Integration bottlenecks with external apps
  - Complexity and limitations making enhancements a high-risk proposition

- **Scenario 2**
  Objectives:

  1. Ensure that customers receive consistent response across products and services internationally
  2. Accurate, complete, timely and consistent data—when, where and how they need it

  Problem Statement:

  - Landscape of many applications that are mix of mainframe, client-server and web-based applications.
  - Most of these systems span all three platforms to support business processes that exchange data synchronously and asynchronously. This makes the support and enhancements difficult and expensive.
  - Some of the applications are so old that the technology used is not supported from the vendor anymore.
  - Communications between systems are mostly created as patch-on solutions rather than real integration, thus resulting in multiple interfaces that are not extensible or scalable.
  - Data delivery through global portals creates the case for upgrading most systems to global applications and standard process platform.

- **Scenario 3**
  Objectives: Enterprise level initiative in banks for transforming operations in order to be able to effectively handle the front-office trade transactions across different geographies.
  Problem Statement:

  - Diverse and obsolete technology platform
  - Non-conformance to industry regulations
  - Heavy manual intervention for trade enrichment
  - Enterprise architecture principles like reusability, scalability not supported
  - Not scalable beyond a certain point, to be able to generate the reports in a small time window
  - Data integrity issues
  - Heavily lacking standardization and governance
  - Limited to serving single geography; does not scale to an enterprise level to support global deployments

- **Scenario 4**
  Objectives: Complicated process and outdated technology resulting in severe performance issues. Improvement to make the architecture scalable and flexible to support current and future business needs of market research companies.
  Problem Statement:

  - Complicated process resulting in large volume of data generation
  - Diverse and obsolete technology platform
  - Old and inadequate infrastructure
  - Redundant manual process
  - Data duplication
  - Interference between online users and offline processes resulting in database dead locks
  - Slow running back-end processes causing bottlenecks in the job queue

- **Scenario 5**
  Objectives: Claims system modernization of insurance companies with existing systems having unduly complex external interfaces resulting in higher maintenance cost and with the application inventory consisting of monolithic claim processing solution, legacy mainframe applications among others.
  Problem Statement:

  - Functionality rationalization across applications
  - Research through the business processes, the mainframe data dictionary and transactions to identify the Business Object Model (BOM) for claim life-cycle solutions
  - Identify data and business services requirement leveraging existing resources from existing claim service ecosystem
  - Define service payloads to optimize service performance
  - Develop service catalog and institutionalize

- **Scenario 6**
  Objectives: Introduce new products/services and go after new markets.
  Problem Statement:

  - Existing architecture very inflexible, with too many point-to-point integrations and highly customized workflow that embedded business logic within it
  - Existing architecture unable to support:
    - o Faster time to market, expansion into new geographies, business growth
    - o Spike in transaction volume
    - o Single customer view across business units
    - o Optimization of business processes and transparency
    - o Compliance with frequent and sudden regulatory changes

- **Scenario 7**
  Objectives: To achieve "Functional Equivalency" of applications in BFSI organizations.
  Problem Statement:

  - Applications developed incrementally over several years with poor or no architectural governance
  - Business critical application does not have any owner
  - Applications or application components do not have source code

- **Scenario 8**
  Objectives: Standardize the architecture and core insurance processes in insurance organizations.
  Problem Statement:
  In a decentralized global operating model, each BU in respective country follows its own approach to architecture and defines core insurance processes. This became a bottleneck in achieving the following aspects:

  - Efficiency in acquiring new business in the market space
  - Customers having challenges to have their policy administration functions performed in a uniform fashion when they own multiple products from the carrier in multiple countries
  - High turnaround time for addressing the requests
  - Disparity in the platforms and processes becoming unmanageable and adding cost to the bottom line

- **Scenario 9**
  Objectives: Key changes in the academic publishing industry, ranging from the shift to digital content/services to free, "good enough" content, are forcing the re-evaluation and optimization in business models and operations.
  Problem Statement:

  - Shift to customized, digital, and mobile content
  - Increasing focus on customer including an evolving definition of "customer"
  - Market and geographic expansion with new business models and new services

- Maturing industry model challenging norms of owning capital assets
- Processes and enterprise systems to address required future business capabilities
- Technology landscape not designed in holistic way
- IT systems with overlapping and duplicate functionality across varied technology
- Point-to-point batch mode integrations

- **Scenario 10**
  Objectives: Global market research firm, consisting of several operating companies formed by merger and acquisition over many years, operating globally.

  - Operating companies encouraged to compete rather than cooperate
  - Several independent and autonomous IT organizations

  Problem Statement:

  - No inter-operating company standards for application architecture and development
  - A proliferation of platforms and middleware
  - Escalating software licensing costs
  - Increasing financial risks due to unsupported hardware / operating systems platforms and little understood software components
  - No reuse of common components
  - No sharing of data or metadata
  - No common services components
  - No service orientation within or across operating companies

- **Scenario 11**
  Objectives: Cohesive small commercial and specialty underwriting capability for P&C (Property & Casualty) Insurers.
  Problem Statement:

  - A proliferation of pinpoint adjunct add-ons to address functional deficiencies in the base application implementation
  - Multitude of interfaces with external applications that were sources and sinks of data with no canonical model for interchange
  - Increasing end-user frustration with lack of functionality and time to market for critical new functionality (leading to erosion of market leadership)

- **Scenario 12**
  Objectives: Capture the current capabilities and processes of major functional units of banks such as Corporate, Finance Complex & Operations.
  Problem Statement:
  A multi-platform IT landscape with high degree of legacy technologies, silos within multiple functional units spanning multiple geographies world-wide, facing challenges with:

  - Lack of visibility of applications providing various business capability and core business functions and risks across enterprise

- Lack of visibility of application life cycle management
- Lack of visibility of technology standards and risks
- Which parts of my business are most at risk?
- Where are my most damaging information-leakage risk areas?
- Lack of governance
- Can we get an enterprise view of what's being used and where?
- Lack of an established model for traceability between various key enterprise architecture concerns (e.g., capability vs. IT investments)

- **Scenario 13**
  Objectives: Create business benefits driven organization for consumer lifestyle and healthcare company and on-going transformation to standardize business processes.
  Problem Statement:

  - The organization's business and IT organizations not completely aligned as IT organization funded independently and business not measured on business benefits accrued from IT projects
  - IT projects not prioritized to fulfill business demands
  - IT road map alignment to business needs not present

- **Scenario 14**
  Objectives: Enterprise-wide strategic, core and support business capabilities for health regulators.
  Problem Statement:

  - Non-existent enterprise architecture practice and elementary understanding of enterprise architecture
  - Lack of integrated view of business capabilities vis-à-vis application, data and technology
  - Fuzzy understanding of as-is business capabilities with respect to organization structure
  - Incomplete and siloed knowledge of technology landscape
  - Inability to carry out impact analysis due to changes / modifications in technology, data or applications
  - No common repository for architectural artifacts

- **Scenario 15**
  Objectives: Enterprise transformation program in retail domain to prepare for the digital tomorrow.
  Problem Statement:

  - The organization has embarked on a transformation journey
  - Some individual initiatives have been identified for consolidation of various systems, upgrade of other systems, etc.
  - The organization has identified that there is lacuna in the holistic planning process of the enterprise

- Strategic enterprise architecture planning exercise is missing to identify end-state and specific initiatives to ensure realization of business vision, goals, objectives
- There is shortcoming in having cogent, overarching enterprise level views

- **Scenario 16**
  Objectives: Achieve alignment, standardization and flexibility at a platform and organizational level in financial services organizations along the four dimensions of business, application, data and technology.
  Problem Statement:

  - A mix of mainframe, client-server, web, middleware and SOA based applications
  - Lack of standardization and common architecture practice across platforms
  - Lack of economic optimization and service, infrastructure reuse
  - Lack of Governance across the enterprise
  - Lack of adoption of common reference architecture

- **Scenario 17**
  Objectives: Achieve alignment, standardization and flexibility at a segment and product level in communications and information technology domain, marked by mix of client-server, web-based applications.
  Problem Statement:

  - Lack of common architecture practice across segments
  - Lack of common technology, common services and infrastructure reuse
  - Lack of standardization and governance across segments

- **Scenario 18**
  Objectives: Rationalize and re-platform IT based on own business vision and goal and streamline data and services in credit profile service organizations, subsequent to M&A.
  Problem Statement:

  - Inherited IT systems from the parent company
  - Major systems such as Sales, CRM (Customer Relationship Management) and Telephony, CMS (Content Management System), etc. and a large number of small applications used by sales force
  - Business processes not optimized due to limitations and integrations issues between the applications
  - Inefficient fulfillment process as customers do not have one-stop solution for purchasing a product
  - Craft newer products with speedy time-to-market based on the data received from multiple sources
  - Conservative average customer spending

- **Scenario 19**
  Objectives: Application suite for decision making in credit rating companies.

Problem Statement:

- Information stored all over the place
- Lack of integrated view of enterprise
- Aligning IT strategies with business needs
- Ensuring multiple artifacts are current
- Control over information assets
- Completeness, consistency and simplification
- Addressing changing stakeholder needs
- Portfolio rationalization

- **Scenario 20**
  Objectives: Setting up enterprise continuum—single 'Living' source of processes and standardized architectural artifacts in financial services institutions with globally dispersed business units, and achieve alignment, standardization and flexibility at a platform and organizational level.
  Problem Statement:

  - Multitude of platforms
  - Mix of mainframe, client–server, web, middleware and SOA based apps
  - Lack of standardization and common reference architecture practice across platforms
  - Lack of economic optimization, service, Infrastructure reuse and governance across the enterprise

- **Scenario 21**
  Objectives: Design strategic solutions to support emerging business needs.
  Problem Statement:

  - Constructive strategic IT solution developments across multi-business units / enterprise and years
  - Traceable and holistic alignment between business strategies and emerging IT solutions development
  - Flexible enterprise architecture model to meet dynamic resource requirement to meet the strategic solution development needs

- **Scenario 22**
  Objectives: Centralize contact center operations for achieving better efficiencies, customer experience and business growth; contact center consolidation, aligning with print and digital subscriptions strategy for a global media company.
  Problem Statement:

  - Geographically distributed business units and contact centers
  - Disparate business processes and legacy technology platforms
  - Lack of solution and approach to centralize the contact centers from divisional locations

- Overall strategy, costs and benefits, approach/plan and change management considerations for implementing the centralized subscription customer service center
- Assessment of current subscriptions-based capabilities and coming up with interim approach
- Come up with integrated subscriber management, consolidated customer view, governance, controls and compliance
- Effective centralized operations, better customer experience and the ability to bundle print and online subscriptions

- **Scenario 23**
  Objectives: Complete renewal of pharmacy offerings for healthcare (pharmacy) organization.
  Problem Statement:

  - A customer centric approach
  - Fulfillment at retail drug store, centralized retail fulfillment, specialty drugs or via home care
  - Delivery options of retail, vending machine or mail
  - Reorganize silos of redundant functionality with adhoc integration paradigms to a more agile Service-Oriented architecture
  - Broad identification of services, their business alignment and realization

- **Scenario 24**
  Objectives: Develop comprehensive set of application blueprints—across siloed business functions, providing a set of views encompassing application functionality, data and implementation (from conceptual, logical and physical perspectives) for banking domain with global operations with regulatory, business, governance & strategic considerations as the main drivers for the blueprinting initiative.
  Problem Statement:

  - Drivers related:
    o Regulators—current state, system interaction, information flow, ownership
    o Business—current state of IT landscape
    o Project team—system interaction, information flow
    o Strategic data andcore framework—information on silo solution
    o Project governance—enterprise alignment, business value
    o EA functions—capture current pain points
  - Scope related—capital market front office business across following silos:
    o Equities
    o eCommerce
    o Fixed Income
    o Currency
    o Commodities
    o Futures

    o Global arbitrage trading

    o Operations

    o Risk

    o Finance

    o Structured Products

- **Scenario 25**
  Objectives: Formulation of integration strategy to address challenges in the IT systems supporting clinical R&D.
  Problem Statement:

  - Each sub-division of clinical R&D have historically procured their own IT applications for needed automation with no attention to collaboration across R&D divisions
  - COTS (commercial off-the-shelf) applications, not readily interoperable with integration standards
  - Various manual processes to enter or copy data from one system to another
  - Business process optimization
  - Standardization of data terminology, semantics, structure
  - Disambiguation of system of record for data entities
  - Improved ability to analyze current and historic data for better business intelligence

- **Scenario 26**
  Objectives:

  1. Representative healthcare major has at least three similar sets of functionalities in the enterprise, as a result of Mergers & Acquisitions, unable to cross-sell and up-sell, thereby taking a toll on its top line and bottom-line.
  2. The multiple IT platforms and other IT deficiencies have resulted in reduced customer satisfaction and higher "IT cost per policy" compared to its peers.

  Problem Statement:
  - A landscape of multitude of applications that can be summarized as:
    - o Functional redundancy
    - o Diverse and obsolete technology platform
    - o Non-conformance to industry regulations
    - o No domain separation
    - o Heavy manual intervention
    - o Extremely poor in implementing "single version of truth"
    - o Data integrity issues
    - o Lacks heavily on standardization and governance

- **Scenario 27**
  Objectives: Portfolio rationalization for representative healthcare organization.

Problem Statement:

- Unable to cross-sell and up-sell which has caused a toll on its top line and bottom line
- Multiple IT platforms and deficiencies have resulted in reduced customer satisfaction
- Diverse and obsolete technology platforms
- No domain separation and heavy manual interventions
- Data integrity issues and lacks on standardization and governance

- **Scenario 28**
  Objectives: Portfolio rationalization and roadmap for representative retail banking services providers.
  Problem Statement:

  - Current IT platforms which are diverse and obsolete have resulted in acquiring expertise, performing upgrades, agility and time to market
  - Reduced customer satisfaction
  - Lack of compatibility with new technologies
  - Lack of standardization and governance

- **Scenario 29**
  Objectives:

  1. Enterprise transformation for representative retail banking service providers with bank assurance products using Enterprise Architecture.
  2. The current IT platforms in several bank assurance segments with obsolete technology platform and other IT deficiencies have resulted in acquiring expertise, performing upgrades, agility, and time-to-market thus increasing TCO (Total Cost of Ownership) and reduced customer satisfaction compared to its peers.

  Problem Statement:
  A landscape of bank assurance products which caters to various segments that can be summarized as:

  - Technology support withdrawn by the technology vendor
  - Acquiring expertise and performing upgrades
  - Diverse and obsolete technology platform
  - Lack of compatibility with new technologies
  - Extremely poor in implementing "single version of truth"
  - Data integrity issues
  - Lacks heavily on standardization and governance

- **Scenario 30**
  Objectives: Implement Integration Infrastructure

Problem Statement:

- Technology landscape has evolved over time and not aligned to holistic design considerations to fulfill enterprise vision and strategic business objectives
- Evolved enterprise having IT systems with overlapping and duplicate functionality across varied technology
- Lacking pan-enterprise view and moving in independent project to project mode
- Point-to-point batch mode integrations

- **Scenario 31**
  Objectives: Improved operations for representative bank holding companies.
  Problem Statement:

  - Expanding enterprise architecture CoE practice across different LOBs (Lines of Business), setting up processes, tools, standards, best practices and guidelines for architecture creation process
  - Setting best practices for architecture creation through standardizing architecture principles, architecture artifacts guideline, templates, methods, stencils and product strategy
  - Creation of standard technology / platform selection guidance process

- **Scenario 32**
  Objectives: Define architecture patterns for pharmacy benefit management organization to consolidate and integrate the IT platforms of acquired organization.
  Problem Statement:
    The pharmacy benefit management organization has acquired other businesses and is in the process of consolidation which posed challenges such as:

  - Lack of transparency and reuse
  - Lack of integrated view or alignment between the different stakeholders
  - Multiplicity of efforts in solution implementation
  - Inability to enforce recommended standards

- **Scenario 33**
  Objectives: Align DFA (Department of Foreign Affairs) compliance and IT policies to longer term business vision in capital markets of large multi-lateral development banks and front to back office process automation and technology landscape analysis, target state definition, solution architecture and roadmap for DFA Compliance in capital markets of large multi-lateral development banks.
  Problem Statement:

  - Trade life-cycle process flows in capital markets are completely manual aided by some internally developed software
  - DFA compliance impact on processes and systems
  - Bringing in the automation in front to back office operations
  - Integration with various systems both internal and external

- Identify and suggest industry best practices in key functions and systems
- Assess the gaps, concerns, regulatory compliance and suggest a solution
- Understand corporate IT policies and suggest the roadmap

- **Scenario 34**
  Objectives: Definition of Enterprise-wide SOA Foundation to standardize people, process, technology and infrastructures for service delivery for premier Sports, Outdoor and lifestyle retailers.
  Problem Statement:

  - Heterogeneous IT systems landscape with higher degree of tactical data integration leading to lower intrinsic interoperability and federation between systems
  - IT inadequately aligned with a formal business architecture leading to redundant IT systems and system of records
  - Lack of a standard, consistent approach or method for service development leading to limited reuse potential of services
  - Lack of enterprise-wide standards for technologies and platforms

- **Scenario 35**
  Objectives: Forecast orders from various export destinations of representative global auto companies. The relevant business unit is the Export Division that supports more than 50 independent distributors in as many countries with their unique market places.
  Problem Statement:

  - Envision new applications to address:
    o Inefficient demand planning process—existing sales, inventory and production planning process (current application—spreadsheets)
    o Manual reports—spreadsheet reports with wasted productivity, limited analytics and human errors
    o Limited supply chain visibility—no visibility to the ocean voyage of the supply
    o Multiple applications, not a single interface for the export business activities

- **Scenario 36**
  Objectives: EA framework definition and development for representative organizations that are sources of commercial information and insight on businesses, having globally dispersed business units, practicing their inhouse architectures and standards; strong need to showcase the relationship between the business process, applications architecture and infrastructure.
  Problem Statement:

  - A landscape of large number of platforms that can be summarized as:
    o Inter-relationships between the enterprise constituents are not defined creating confusion
    o Lack of standardization and common architecture practice across platforms
    o Lack of economic optimization andservice, infrastructure reuse
    o Lack of governance across the enterprise

- **Scenario 37**
  Objectives: Enterprise architecture strategy definition
  Problem Statement:

  - Existing landscape can be summarized as:
    o Technology landscape not designed in holistic way to fulfill enterprise vision and strategic business objectives
    o Evolved enterprise having IT systems with overlapping and duplicate functionality across varied technology
    o Lacking pan-enterprise view
    o Point-to-point batch mode integrations

- **Scenario 38**
  Objectives: Enterprise Architecture strategy for representative legacy insurance companies with large number of employees, many independent agents.
  Problem Statement:

  - Challenges faced by the team can be summarized thus:
    o Legacy systems with scarce documentation and unduly complex external interfaces resulting in higher maintenance cost
    o The application inventory consists of disparate claim processing solutions, amongst others
    o Ensure functionality rationalization including user interfaces

- **Scenario 39**
  Objectives: Application portfolio management to save costs through rationalization and standardization of business technology assets for representative insurance groups, with thousands of employees serving customers globally.
  Problem Statement:
  Business Technology landscape spread across Europe, LATAM, APAC, ME and North America with multiple business segments spanning multiple business units, 3500+ applications with:

  - Lack of visibility of application life cycle management
  - Lack of technology standardization
  - Lack of visibility in IT spending and investment
  - Lack of governance across the enterprise
  - No single source of truth for application portfolio management

- **Scenario 40**
  Objectives: Enterprise Architecture driven cost transparency and cost control for representative business process and document management organizations.
  Problem Statement:

  - Challenges in cost transparency and cost control
  - Challenged to find answer to the following questions:

    o End Customer audits—how do we achieve real time access to information enabling fast, accurate answers?

    o Can we get an enterprise view of what's being used and where?

    o What is the cost incurred in delivering the services to the end customer?

- **Scenario 41**

  Objectives: Ensure business and technology investment is in alignment with business goals and strategy, through governance process and effective enterprise portfolio management, for representative global insurance & reinsurance groups, with diversified market place and multi-platform approach serving customers worldwide.

  Problem Statement:

  Europe, Bermuda, US serving multiple business segments spanning multiple business units world-wide facing challenges with:

  - Lack of visibility of application providing various capability and business functions and risks across enterprise
  - Lack of visibility in IT spending and capability investment
  - Where am I spending my Opex / Capex budgets?
  - Lack of visibility of application life cycle management
  - Lack of visibility of technology standards and risks
  - Which parts of my business are most at risk?
  - Where are my most damaging information-leakage risk areas?
  - Lack of governance
  - Can we get an enterprise view of what's being used and where?

- **Scenario 42**

  Objectives: Blueprint enterprise architecture of segmented BUs for business, application, information, technology and inter-relationships across segments for representative information and benchmark insights and publishing organizations.

  Problem Statement:

  Business technology landscape with multiple platforms spread globally serving multiple business segments spanning business units worldwide facing challenges with:

  - Enable innovation, standardization and reusable technology solutions for better business–technology alignment
  - Transforming IT to "Business of IT" by aligning with strategic objectives and increasing operational effectiveness

- **Scenario 43**

  Objectives: Policy administration system definition for representative providers of insurance, annuities and employee benefit programs across the world.

  Problem Statement:

  - Recurring defects and high number of change requests
  - Back-end data patching
  - Frequent system outages

- Increase in manual workaround
- Lack of adequate compliance
- Decide whether to retain or replace the current policy admin system
- Understand what changes need to be made to the policy admin system to make it responsive to business needs as well as alleviate the current set of business issues and challenges

- **Scenario 44**
  Objectives: Digital Transformation for representative banks with the objective of moving toward next generation banking.
  Problem Statement:

  - The application portfolio has evolved over a period of time resulting in lack of standardized architecture
  - Legacy applications used for key business processes resulting in increased time to market for a product
  - Integration bottlenecks
  - Complexity and limitations making enhancements a high-risk proposition

References

1. Goncalo Candido, Jose Barata, Armando Walter Colombo, and Francois Jammes, SOA in reconfigurable supply chains: A research roadmap, *Engineering Applications of Artificial Intelligence*, 22 (2009) 939–949.
2. Marco Crasso, Alejandro Zunino, and Marcelo Campo, Easy web service discovery: A query-by-example approach, *Science of Computer Programming*, 71 (2008) 144–164.
3. Omar El-Gayar, and Kanchana Tandekar, An XML-based schema definition for model sharing and reuse in a distributed environment, *Decision Support Systems*, 43 (2007) 791–808.
4. Chua Fang Fang, and Lee Chien Sing, Collaborative learning using service-oriented architecture: A framework design, *Knowledge-Based Systems*, 22 (2009) 271–274.
5. Tae-Young Kim, Sunjae Lee, Kwangsoo Kim, and Cheol-Han Kim, A modeling framework for agile and interoperable virtual enterprises, *Computers in Industry*, 57 (2006) 204–217.
6. Marcos L'opez-Sanz, Cesar J. Acuna, Carlos E. Cuesta, and Esperanza Marcos, Modelling of Service-Oriented Architectures with UML, *Electronic Notes in Theoretical Computer Science*, 194 (2008) 23–37.
7. David Chen, Guy Doumeingts, and Francois Vernadat, Architectures for enterprise integration and interoperability: Past, present and future, *Computers in Industry*, 59 (2008) 647–659.
8. Claudia-Melania Chituc, Americo Azevedo, and Cesar Toscano, A framework proposal for seamless interoperability in a collaborative networked environment, *Computers in Industry*, 60 (2009) 317–338.
9. Karim Baına, Khalid Benali, and Claude Godart, DISCOBOLE: A service architecture for interconnecting workflow processes, *Computers in Industry*, 57 (2006) 768–777.
10. Daniela Grigori, Fabio Casati, Malu Castellanos, Umeshwar Dayal, Mehmet Sayal, and Ming-Chien Shan, Business process intelligence, *Computers in Industry*, 53 (2004) 321–343.
11. Ricardo Jardim-Goncalves, Antonio Grilo, and Adolfo Steiger-Garcao, Challenging the interoperability between computers in industry with MDA and SOA, *Computers in Industry*, 57 (2006) 679–689.
12. Y. Rezgui, Role-based service-oriented implementation of a virtual enterprise: A case study in the construction sector, *Computers in Industry*, 58 (2007) 74–86.
13. Yanbo Han, Jing Wang, and Peng Zhang, Business-oriented service modeling: A case study, *Simulation Modelling Practice and Theory*, 17 (2009) 1413–1429.
14. Debasis Chanda, Dwijesh Dutta Majumder, and Swapan Bhattacharya, *"Virtual consolidation: A new paradigm of service oriented distributed architecture for indian banking system"*, *Proceedings of International Conference on Emerging Applications of Information Technology, Elsevier*, pp. 57–62, Kolkata (2006).
15. Easwaran G Nadhan, *"Service-Oriented Architecture: Implementation Challenges"*, White Work (2004). www.microsoft.com.
16. Kishore Channabasavaiah, Kernie Holley, IBM Global Services, Edward M. Tuggle, Jr., and IBM Software Group, *"Migrating to a Service-Oriented Architecture"*, White Work (2004) www.ibm.com.
17. T.T. Ram Mohan, Bank consolidation: Issues and evidence, *Economic and Political Weekly* (2005) 1151–1161.
18. Rupa Rege Nitsure, *"Basel II norms: Emerging market perspective with Indian focus"*, *Economic and Political Weekly*, 40 (2005) 1162–1166.
19. B. Esra Aslanertik, Enabling integration to create value through process-based management accounting systems, *International Journal of Value Chain Management*, 1, 3 (2007) 223–238.
20. Salah Baı̈na, Hervé Panetto, and Gérard Morel, New paradigms for a product oriented modelling: Case study for traceability, *Computers in Industry*, 60 (2009) 172–183.

21. Kuo-Ming Chao, Muhammad Younas, and Nathan Griffiths, BPEL4WS-based coordination of Grid Services in design, *Computers in Industry*, 57 (2006) 778–786.

22. Tsung-Yi Chen, Yuh-Min Chen, Hui-Chuan Chu, and Chin-Bin Wang, Development of an access control model, system architecture and approaches for resource sharing in virtual enterprise, *Computers in Industry*, 58 (2007) 57–73.

23. Yahui Lu, Li Zhang, and Jiaguang Sun, Task-activity based access control for process collaboration environments, *Computers in Industry*, 60 (2009) 403–415.

24. Valentín Valero, M. Emilia Cambronero, Gregorio Díaz, and Hermenegilda Macià, A Petri net approach for the design and analysis of web services choreographies, *The Journal of Logic and Algebraic Programming*, 78 (2009) 359–380.

25. Chun Ouyang, Eric Verbeek, Wil M.P. van der Aalst, Stephan Breutel, Marlon Dumas, and Arthur H.M. ter Hofstede, Formal semantics and analysis of control flow in WS-BPEL, *Science of Computer Programming*, 67 (2007) 162–198.

26. Niels Lohmann, Peter Massuthe, Christian Stahl, and Daniela Weinberg, Analyzing interacting WS-BPEL processes using flexible model generation, *Data & Knowledge Engineering*, 64 (2008) 38–54.

27. Manu De Backer, Monique Snoeck, Geert Monsieur, Wilfried Lemahieu, and Guido Dedene, A scenario-based verification technique to assess the compatibility of collaborative business processes, *Data & Knowledge Engineering*, 68 (2009) 531–551.

28. Remi Bastide, and Eric Barboni, Software components: A formal semantics based on coloured petri nets, *Electronic Notes in Theoretical Computer Science*, 160 (2006) 57–73.

29. King Sing Cheung, T.Y. Cheung, and K.O. Chow, A petri-net-based synthesis methodology for use-case-driven system design, *The Journal of Systems and Software*, 79 (2006) 772–790.

30. Hartmut Ehrig, Kathrin Hoffmann, and Julia Padberg, Transformations of Petri Nets, *Electronic Notes in Theoretical Computer Science*, 148 (2006) 151–172.

31. Dragan Gasevic, and Vladan Devedzic, Petri net ontology, *Knowledge-Based Systems*, 19 (2006) 220–234.

32. Seungchul Ha, and Hyo-Won Suh, A timed colored Petri nets modeling for dynamic workflow in product development process, *Computers in Industry*, 59 (2008) 193–209.

33. Stephane Julia, Fernanda Francielle de Oliveira, and Robert Valette, Real time scheduling of Workflow Management Systems based on a p-time Petri net model with hybrid resources, *Simulation Modelling Practice and Theory*, 16 (2008) 462–482.

34. Wil M.P. van der Aalst, Business process management demystified: A tutorial on models, systems and standards for workflow management, *Lectures on Concurrency and Petri Nets*, 2003 1–65.

35. Nick Russell, Arthur H.M. ter Hofstede, Wil M.P. van der Aalst, and Nataliya Mulyar, Workflow Control-Flow Patterns A Revised View, *BPM Center Report BPM-06-22* (2006). BPMcenter.org.

36. Wil van der Aalst, and Kees van Hee *"Workflow Management: Models, Methods, and Systems"*, (2002) MIT Press.

37. Zouhua Ding, Horst Bunke, Moti Schneider, and Abraham Kandel, Fuzzy timed Petri net — definitions, properties and applications, *Mathematical and Computer Modelling*, 41 (2005) 345–360.

38. Julia Padberg, and Hartmut Ehrig, Petri net modules in the transformation-based component framework, *The Journal of Logic and Algebraic Programming*, 67 (2006) 198–225.

39. Julia Padberg, Petri net modules, *Journal on Integrated Design and Process Technology*, 6 (4) (2002) 105–120.

40. H. Ehrig, F. Orejas, B. Braatz, M. Klein, and M. Piirainen, *A generic component concept for system modeling*, in: *Proceedings of FASE '02, Lecture Notes in Computer Science*, 2306 Springer (2002).

41. Fernando Rosa-Velardo, Olga Marroquín-Alonso, and David de Frutos-Escrig, Mobile Synchronizing Petri Nets: A Choreographic Approach for Coordination in Ubiquitous Systems, *Electronic Notes in Theoretical Computer Science*, 150 (2006) 103–126.

42. James Rambaugh, Michael Blaha, William Premerlani, Frederich Eddy, and William Lorensen, *"Object Oriented Modeling and Design,"* (2005), Pearson Education.

43. Mark Priestley, *"Practical Object Oriented Design with UML,"* (2005) Tata McGraw-Hill Publishing Company Ltd., 2nd Edition.

44. Hans Koehler Ulrich Nickel, Jörg Niere, and Albert Zuendorf, *"Integrating UML diagrams for production control systems",* IEEE Computer Society, *Proceedings of the 22nd Annual Conference on Software Engineering,* 241–251 (2000).

45. http://en.wikipedia.org/wiki/Activity_diagram.

46. Michael Andersson, Anders Ek, and Niklas Landin, Utilizing UML in SDL-based Development, *Computer Networks,* 35 (2001) 613–625.

47. K. Benghazi Akhlaki, M. I. Capel Tuñón, J.A. Holgado Terriza, and L.E. Mendoza Morales, A methodological approach to the formal specification of real-time systems by transformation of UML-RT design models, *Science of Computer Programming,* 65 (2007) 41–56.

48. Daniela Berardi, Diego Calvanese, and Giuseppe De Giacomo, Reasoning on UML class diagrams, *Artificial Intelligence,* 168 (2005) 70–118.

49. Kirsten Berkenk"otter, Reliable UML models and profiles, *Electronic Notes in Theoretical Computer Science,* 217 (2008) 203–220.

50. Rafael Magalh~aes Borges, and Alexandre Cabral Mota, Integrating UML and formal methods, *Electronic Notes in Theoretical Computer Science,* 184 (2007) 97–112.

51. Thouraya Bouabana-Tebibel, and Mounira Belmesk, An object-oriented approach to formally analyze the UML 2.0 activity partitions, *Information and Software Technology,* 49 (2007) 999–1016.

52. Patr'ıcia Ferreira, Augusto Sampaio, and Alexandre Mota, Viewing CSP specifications with UML-RT diagrams, *Electronic Notes in Theoretical Computer Science,* 195 (2008) 57–74.

53. Chanan Glezer, Mark Last, Efrat Nachmany, and Peretz Shoval, Quality and comprehension of UML interaction diagrams-an experimental comparison, *Information and Software Technology,* 47 (2005) 675–692.

54. Martin Grossman, Jay E. Aronson, and Richard V. McCarthy, Does UML make the grade? Insights from the software development community, *Information and Software Technology,* 47 (2005) 383–397.

55. Karsten Ho" lscher, Paul Ziemann, and Martin Gogolla, On translating UML models into graph transformation systems, *Journal of Visual Languages and Computing,* 17 (2006) 78–105.

56. Ali Kamandi, Mohammad Abdollahi Azgomi, and Ali Movaghar, Transformation of UML Models into Analyzable OSAN Models, *Electronic Notes in Theoretical Computer Science,* 159 (2006) 3–22.

57. Jun Kong, Kang Zhang, Jing Dong, and Dianxiang Xu, Specifying behavioral semantics of UML diagrams through graph transformations, *The Journal of Systems and Software,* 82 (2009) 292–306.

58. Francisco J. Lucas, Fernando Molina, and Ambrosio Toval, A systematic review of UML model consistency management, *Information and Software Technology,* 51 (2009) 1631–1645.

59. Ariadi Nugroho, and Michel R.V. Chaudron, *A survey into the rigor of UML use and its perceived impact on quality and productivity,* in: ESEM'08: *Proceedings of the Second ACM-IEEE International Symposium on Empirical Software Engineering and Measurement,* ACM, New York, NY, USA, 2008, pp. 90–99.

60. Ariadi Nugroho, and Michel R.V. Chaudron, Managing the quality of UML models in practice, in: J. Rech, C. Bunse (Eds.), *Model-Driven Software Development: Integrating Quality Assurance, Information Science Reference,* IGI Publishing, Hershey, PA, 2008, pp. 1–36 (Chapter 1).

61. Christian F.J. Lange, Michel R.V. Chaudron, and Johan Muskens, In practice: UML software architecture and design description, *IEEE Software,* 23 (2) (2006) 40–46.

62. Ariadi Nugroho, Level of detail in UML models and its impact on model comprehension: A controlled experiment, *Information and Software Technology,* 51, 12 (December 2009) 1670–1685.

63. Paul Ziemann, Karsten H"olscher, and Martin Gogolla, Coherently explaining UML statechart and collaboration diagrams by graph transformations, *Electronic Notes in Theoretical Computer Science,* 130 (2005) 263–280.

64. Claus Pahl, Semantic model-driven architecting of service-based software systems, *Information and Software Technology,* 49 (2007) 838–850.

65. Sinuhe Arroyo, Miguel-Angel Sicilia, and Juan-Manuel Dodero, Choreography frameworks for business integration: Addressing heterogeneous semantics, *Computers in Industry*, 58 (2007) 487–503.

66. Harinder Jagdev, Laurentiu Vasiliu, Jim Browne, and Michal Zaremba, A semantic web service environment for B2B and B2C auction applications within extended and virtual enterprises, *Computers in Industry*, 59 (2008) 786–797.

67. Jisoo Jung, Injun Choi, and Minseok Song, An integration architecture for knowledge management systems and business process management systems, *Computers in Industry*, 58 (2007) 21–34.

68. George F Luger, *"AI Structures and Strategies for Complex Problem Solving,"* (2006), Pearson Education, 4th Edition.

69. Dirk Beyer, Andreas Noack, and Claus Lewerentz, "Efficient Relational Calculation for Software analysis", *IEEE Transactions on Software Engineering*, 31, 2 (2005) 137–149.

70. Te Fu Chen, The creation and operation of knowledge-based innovation networks in high-tech SME's, *Journal of Knowledge Management Practice*, 9, 4 (December 2008).

71. Khalid Samara, Dilip Patel, and Shushma Patel, An ontology based knowledge experiential learning framework, *Journal of Knowledge Management Practice*, 8, 3 (September 2007).

72. Karina Rodriguez, and Ahmed Al-Ashaab, Knowledge web-based system architecture for collaborative product development, *Computers in Industry*, 56 (2005) 125–140.

73. Debasis Chanda, Dwijesh Dutta Majumder, and Swapan Bhattacharya, *"Consolidation of UML diagrams: An AI based solution for bank merger issues"*, Accepted in *CATA-2007 (International Conference on Computers and Their Applications)*, Honolulu, Hawaii, USA (2007).

74. Debasis Chanda, Dwijesh Dutta Majumder, and Swapan Bhattacharya, *"Service oriented process modeling & composition: An AI based architecture"*, Accepted in *18th International Conference on Information Systems Development (ISD2009)*, Nanchang, China (September 16–19, 2009).

75. Debasis Chanda, Dwijesh Dutta Majumder, and Swapan Bhattacharya, *"Service Oriented Architecture: An AI Based Approach"*, Accepted in *WORLDCOMP'09 (World Congress in Computer Science Computer Engineering & Allied Computing): SERP 2009 (Software Engineerin Research & Practice)*, Las Vegas Nevada (July 13–16, 2009).

76. Debasis Chanda, Dwijesh Dutta Majumder, and Swapan Bhattacharya, *"Knowledge Based Business Process Modeling"*, *Proceedings of International Conference on Business & IT* (ICBIRD 2010), Macmillan Advanced Research Series, 66–119, IMT Ghaziabad, February 25–26, 2010.

77. Debasis Chanda, Dwijesh Dutta Majumder, and Swapan Bhattacharya, *"Knowledge based consolidation of uml diagrams for creation of virtual enterprise"*, *Intelligent Information Management*, 2 (2010) 159–177.

78. J.B. Simha, and S.S. Iyengar *"Fuzzy data mining for customer loyalty analysis"*, *9th International Conference on Information Technology*, 200, 6 18–21 December 2006 245–246.

79. Qingzhan Chen, Han Jianghong, Wenxiu He, Keji Mao, and Yungang Lai *"Utilize fuzzy data mining to find the travel pattern of browsers"*, *The Fifth International Conference on Computer and Information Technology*, 2005. CIT 2005, 21–23 Sept. 2005, 228–232.

80. R. B. V. Subramanyam, and A. Goswami *"A fuzzy data mining algorithm for incremental mining of quantitative sequential patterns"*, *International Journal of Uncertainty, Fuzziness and Knowledge-Based Systems*, 13, 6 (December 2005) 633–652.

81. Jiawei Han, and Micheline Kamber *"Datamining Concepts and Techniques"*, (2001), Morgan Kaufmann Publishers, San Francisco.

82. Guizhen Yang, *The complexity of mining maximal frequent itemsets and maximal frequent patterns*, *Proceedings of the tenth ACM SIGKDD international conference on Knowledge discovery and data mining*, Seattle (August 22–25, 2004).

83. Hai Jin, Jianhua Sun, Hao Chen, and Zongfen Han *"A Fuzzy Data Mining Based Intrusion Detection Model"*, *10th IEEE International Workshop on Future Trends of Distributed Computing Systems (FTDCS'04)*, 191–197.

84. Wei-Shen Tai, and Chen-Tung Chen *"A Web User Preference Perception System Based on Fuzzy Data Mining Method"*, *Information Retrieval Technology, Lecture Notes in Computer Science*, 4182 (2006).

85. Bernadette Bouchon-Meunier, *"Similarity Management for Fuzzy Data Mining"*, *International Conference on Intelligent Systems and Knowledge Engineering (ISKE 2007)* (2007).

86. Yi-Chung Hu, A new fuzzy-data mining method for pattern classification by principal component analysis, *Cybernetics and Systems*, 36, 5 (July–August 2005), 527–547 (21).

87. Mu-Jung Huang, Yee-Lin Tsoua and Show-Chin Lee *"Integrating fuzzy data mining and fuzzy artificial neural networks for discovering implicit knowledge"*, (2006), Elsevier.

88. Sean N. Ghazavi, and Thunshun W. Liao Medical data mining by fuzzy modeling with selected features, *Artificial Intelligence in Medicine*, 2008,43 (3):195–206.

89. Angryk, R.A. *"Similarity-driven Defuzzification of Fuzzy Tuples for Entropy-based Data Classification Purposes"*, *2006 IEEE International Conference on Fuzzy Systems*, (2006) 414–422.

90. Ding-An Chiang, Louis R. Chow, and Yi-Fan Wang *"Mining time series data by a fuzzy linguistic summary system"*, *Fuzzy Sets and Systems*, 112, 3 (2000) 419–432.

91. Dwijesh Dutta Majumder, and Debasis Chanda *"Datamining & knowledge discovery using a fuzzy mathematical approach for the indian agricultural system management"*, *Fuzzy Logic and Its Application in Technology and Management*, Narosa Publishing House (June 2006) 73–80.

92. Dwijesh Dutta Majumder, and Debasis Chanda *"Study on a Framework for Agricultural Forecasting Systems An application of Information Technology & Datamining Techniques in the Indian Scenario"* Presented in an International Conference on *"Recent Trends & New Directions of Research in Cybernetics & Systems Theory"*, IASST, Guwahati, India (January 2004).

93. Dwijesh Dutta Majumder, and Sanka K Pal *"Fuzzy Mathematical Approach to Pattern Recognition"*, (1986) John Wiley & Sons (Halsted), N. Y..

94. George J Klir, and Bo Yuan *"Fuzzy Sets and Fuzzy Logic Theory and Applications"*, (2002), Prentice-Hall of India Private Limited, New Delhi.

95. Pieter Adriaans and Dolf Zantinge *"Datamining"*, (1996), Addison-Wesley Professional.

96. Abraham Silberschatz, Henry K. Forth, and S Sudarshan *"Database System Concepts"*, (2002), McGraw Hill, International Edition.

97. Canara Bank Annual Report 2017.

98. Business Standard, Banking Annual 2004.

99. Debasis Chanda, Dwijesh Dutta Majumder, and Swapan Bhattacharya, *"Knowledge Based Service Oriented Architecture for M&A"*, Accepted for Publication in SEKE 2010 (*The 22nd Conference on Software Engineering and Knowledge Engineering*), San Francisco Bay, USA, July 1–3, 2010.

100. Jiawei Han, *"Data Mining: Concepts and Techniques,"* (2005), Morgan Kaufmann Publishers Inc., San Francisco, CA.

101. Zouhua Ding, Horst Bunke, Oscar Kipersztok, Mti Schneider, and Abraham Kandel, Fuzzy timed Petri nets— analysis and implementation, *Mathematical and Computer Modelling*, 43 (2006) 385–400.

Index

9780367720902